Singapore MATH CHALLENGE

W9-CNK-154

GRADE 5+

WORD PROBLEMS

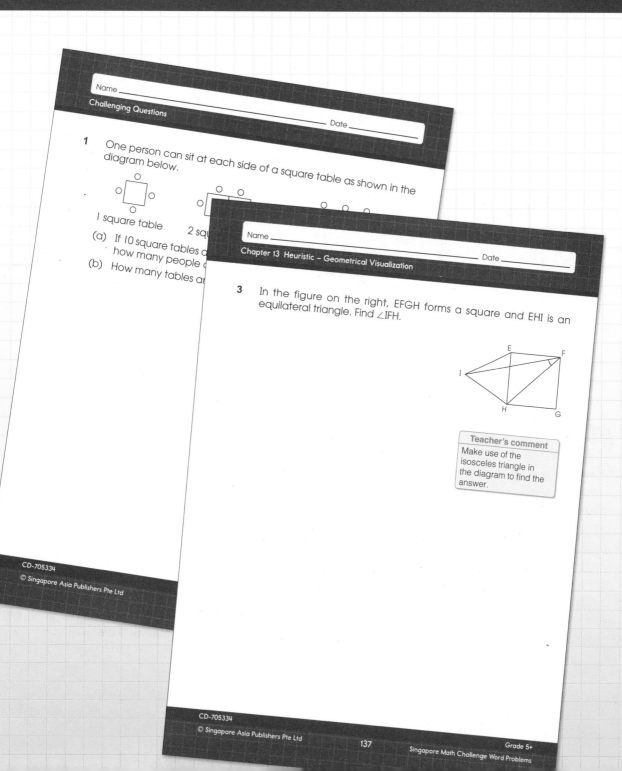

Name _____

Date _____

1   One person can sit at each side of a square table as shown in the diagram below.

I square table   2 squ

(a) If 10 square tables a
      how many people c

(b) How many tables ar

Name _____

Date _____

3   In the figure on the right, EFGH forms a square and EHI is an equilateral triangle. Find ∠IFH.

Teacher's comment

Make use of the isosceles triangle in the diagram to find the answer.

CD-705334
© Singapore Asia Publishers Pte Ltd

Visit carsondellosa.com for correlations to Common Core, state, national, and Canadian provincial standards.

Copyright © 2019 Singapore Asia Publishers Pte. Ltd.

Carson Dellosa Education
PO Box 35665
Greensboro, NC 27425 USA

Printed in the USA • All rights reserved.   ISBN 978-1-4838-5413-7
01-084197784

Table of Contents

LETTER TO PARENTS

In *Singapore Math Challenge Word Problems*, your child will find a variety of intriguing problems and problem-solving methods. Using the tips and tricks offered, solving these word problems will help your child develop skill and creativity as a mathematical thinker.

What is Singapore Math?

Singapore's math curriculum has been recognized worldwide for its excellence in producing students highly skilled in mathematics. Students in Singapore regularly rank at the top of the world in mathematics on the Trends in International Mathematics and Science Study (TIMSS).

The Singapore Math curriculum aims to help students develop necessary concepts and skills for everyday life and to provide students with the ability to formulate, apply, and solve problems. The Singapore Primary (Elementary) Mathematics curriculum covers fewer topics, but in greater depth. Key concepts are introduced and built-on to reinforce mathematical ideas and thinking. Skills are typically taught a full year ahead of when similar skills are taught in the United States.

Singapore Math and the Common Core State Standards

Common Core State Standards in mathematics have been adopted by most U.S. states. These standards are designed to help prepare American students for success in college and in the global twenty-first century workforce. They outline clear, consistent, and rigorous expectations for learning in math.

In developing the Common Core State Standards, experts looked at educationally high-performing nations such as Singapore to identify the best approaches to learning. Singapore math standards are frequently cited in the research used to support the Common Core standards.

Common Core State Standards have raised the bar for American students. Strategies taught in Singapore Math Challenge will help students meet these new expectations.

1 6 years ago, the sum of Jeremy, Quan, Karen, and Randy's age was 20. Find their total age now.

> **Teacher's comment**
> Each person's age must increase by the same number of years.

2 The sum of Jeremy, Quan, and Randy's present age is 38. Find their total age 4 years ago.

3   The sum of Kaden and Tom's present age is 30. In how many years will their total age be 40 years?

4   Jeremy is twice as old as Randy now. 6 years ago, the sum of their age was 18. How old is Jeremy now?

> **Teacher's comment**
>
> Their age difference remains the same.

5 Kaden is $\frac{1}{4}$ as old as Tom now. In 7 years, the sum of their age will be 54. How old is Tom now?

6 10 years ago, the ratio of Jeremy's age to Randy's age to Kaden's age was 4 : 3 : 1. The sum of their present age is 102. Find Randy's age now.

7 Kaden and Quan had a total of 46 marbles at first. After Kaden bought another 10 marbles, they had an equal number of marbles.

(a) How many marbles did Kaden have in the end?

(b) How many marbles did Kaden have at first?

Teacher's comment
First, find the total number of marbles they had in the end. Then, work backward to find the number of marbles Kaden had at first.

8 Ken and Tricia had a total of 81 marbles at first. After Ken lost 11 marbles and Tricia bought another 6 marbles, Ken had three times as many marbles as Tricia. How many marbles did Ken have at first?

9 Angela and Lamar had a total of 41 stickers at first. After Angela lost 5 of her stickers and Lamar lost $\frac{1}{2}$ of his stickers, they had an equal number of stickers left. How many stickers did Lamar have at first?

10 Gabriel and James had a total of 40 toy cars at first. After Gabriel bought another 16 toy cars and James lost $\frac{2}{5}$ of his toy cars, they had an equal number of toy cars left. How many toy cars did Gabriel have at first?

1 Kelvin and Daniel had an equal number of erasers at first. Kelvin gave 4 erasers away and Daniel received another 7 erasers from his brother. How many more erasers did Daniel have than Kelvin in the end?

> **Teacher's comment**
>
> By using model drawing, we will be able to see how many more erasers Daniel had than Kelvin.

2   Kaden and Dave had an equal number of cookies. If Kaden ate 7 cookies and Dave ate 5 cookies, how many more cookies did Dave have than Kaden in the end?

3 Jack and Jill had an equal number of books at first. After Jack borrowed another 20 books and Jill sold 15 books, Jack had 6 times as many books as Jill.

(a) How many more books did Jack have than Jill in the end?

(b) How many books did Jack have in the end?

Teacher's comment
Use model drawing to find out how many more books Jack had. It will also show how many books each unit represents.

4   Kelvin and Daniel had an equal number of paper clips at first. After Kelvin gave away 17 paper clips and Daniel gave away 5 paper clips, Daniel had 5 times as many paper clips as Kelvin. How many paper clips did Daniel have at first?

5 Kaden and Dave bought some stamps and shared them equally between themselves. Mother then gave 1 stamp to Kaden and 9 stamps to Dave. As a result, Kaden had $\frac{3}{5}$ as many stamps as Dave. How many stamps did Kaden and Dave buy altogether?

Teacher's comment
Draw 3 units for Kaden and 5 units for Dave in the model.

6   Nathan had $\frac{4}{7}$ as many pens as Henry at first. After Nathan bought 19 more pens and Henry gave away 8 pens, they had an equal number of pens in the end. How many pens did Nathan have at first?

7 Silas had some money at first. His mother gave him another $6 and he spent $20 on a book. As a result, the ratio of the money he had at first to the money he had in the end was 10 : 3.

(a) Find the difference between the amount of money Silas had at first and the amount of money Silas had in the end.

(b) How much money did Silas have at first?

Teacher's comment
Use the ratio given as units in the model drawing.

8   Lily and Bella had an equal number of dolls at first. Iris had 5 more dolls than Lily. After Bella gave away 10 dolls and Iris gave away 9 dolls, Bella had $\frac{2}{5}$ as many dolls as Iris. How many dolls did Lily have?

9   Kaden had $4 more than Ben. Ben had $7 more than Dan. After Mother gave Kaden $20 and Dan spent $1 on a pen, Kaden had 9 times as much money as Dan. How much did Kaden have at first?

10 Chloe and Sam had an equal number of apples at first. Chloe bought 3 more apples and Sam bought 23 more apples. Chloe then had 60% as many apples as Sam. How many apples did Sam have at first?

1 Robin had 4 times as much money as Shawn at first. After spending some money, Robin realized that Shawn had twice as much as he had. If Robin had $48 at first, how much did Robin have in the end?

2 Reuben had 4 times as much money as Steven at first. After spending some money, Reuben realized that Steven had three times as much as he had. If Steven had $18, how much did Reuben spend?

3   Roy had 5 times as much money as Shane. Roy spent $54 and Shane had twice as much as Roy in the end. How much did Roy have at first?

> **Teacher's comment**
> Cut the units in the model drawing into smaller parts.

4 Ruby had 5 times as much money as Sally. Ruby spent $80 and Sally had $\frac{3}{7}$ as much as Ruby in the end. How much did Ruby have at first?

> **Teacher's comment**
>
> Use the fraction given to cut the model drawing into equal parts for Ruby and Sally.

5 Andy had $240. He had twice as much money as Carl. Carl spent some money and Andy had 6 times as much money as Carl in the end. How much did Carl spend?

6 Bob had $\frac{3}{4}$ as much money as Dan. Dan received another $15. As a result, Bob had $\frac{6}{11}$ as much money as Dan. How much did Dan have at first?

Teacher's comment
The number of units Bob had should remain the same.

7   Calvin had $\frac{1}{2}$ as much money as Eddy. Calvin spent \$36 and Eddy had 8 times as much money as Calvin in the end. How much did both of them have altogether at first?

8   Donnie had $\frac{3}{4}$ as much money as Freda. Donnie spent $63 and Freda had 6 times as much money as Donnie in the end. How much did Freda have?

9   The ratio of the number of tables to chairs at a café was 1 : 4. After the café owner bought 16 more chairs, the ratio of the number of tables to chairs at the café became 3 : 14. How many more chairs than tables were there at the café at first?

10 20% of the passengers on a bus were children. After 10 adults got off the bus, the percentage of children on the bus increased to 30%. How many passengers were on the bus in the end?

1 Christopher and Andy had 200 stamps. Christopher bought another 21 stamps and Andy gave his brother 21 stamps. As a result, Christopher and Andy had the same number of stamps.

(a) How many stamps did they have altogether in the end?

(b) How many stamps did Andy have at first?

2 Christopher and Andy had 300 stamps. Christopher gave 10 stamps to Andy. As a result, Christopher had five times as many stamps as Andy. How many stamps did Andy have at first?

3   Christopher and Andy had 207 stamps. Christopher bought another 12 stamps and Andy gave his brother 12 stamps. As a result, Christopher had $\frac{1}{2}$ as many stamps as Andy. How many stamps did Andy have at first?

4   Alice and Don shared 60 apples. Alice had twice as many apples as Don. When Don gave some apples to Alice, she had four times as many apples as Don.

   (a) How many apples did Don have at first?
   (b) How many apples did Don give Alice?

5 There were $\frac{2}{3}$ as many children as adults on a bus. When 12 children got off the bus and 12 adults boarded, the number of children became $\frac{1}{9}$ the number of adults on the bus. How many adults were on the bus at first?

> **Teacher's comment**
> The total number of passengers on the bus remained the same.

6   Alice and Don shared some apples. Alice had twice as many apples as Don. When Don gave 10 apples to Alice, she had 8 times as many apples as Don in the end. Find the number of apples Alice had at first.

7 The ratio of apples Alice, Ben, and Don had was 3 : 8 : 1. When Ben gave some of his apples to Alice and Don, all of them had the same number of apples in the end. If they had 48 apples in total, how many apples did Don receive from Ben?

Teacher's comment
Divide the apples equally to find out how many apples each person had.

8   The ratio of apples Alice, Ben, and Don had was 3 : 8 : 4. When Ben gave 21 apples to Alice and Don, all of them have the same number of apples in the end. How many apples did Ben have at first?

9 The ratio of Alice's apples to Don's apples was 3 : 5. When Alice gave 30 of her apples to Don, the ratio of Alice's apples to Don's apples became 1 : 5. Find the number of apples Alice had at first.

10 Amy had 25% as many marbles as Ben. After Ben gave some of his marbles to Amy, Amy now has $\frac{3}{7}$ as many marbles as Ben. What fraction of the marbles that he had at first did Ben give to Amy?

1 There are 70 cookies in a box. The number of raisin cookies was $\frac{1}{4}$ the number of plain cookies. Chantalle ate 3 raisin cookies and 3 plain cookies. Find the difference between the number of raisin and plain cookies in the box in the end.

2   There were 60 cookies in a box. The number of raisin cookies was $\frac{1}{3}$ the number of plain cookies. Chantalle ate an equal number of raisin and plain cookies. Find the difference between the number of raisin and plain cookies in the end.

Teacher's comment
When the same number of cookies was subtracted, the number difference remain the same.

3 Kaden is 18 years older than Sally now. In 5 years, Kaden will be 3 times as old as Sally. How old is Sally now?

Teacher's comment

The age difference does not change over the years.

4   When Zoe was 36 years old, her daughter was $\frac{1}{3}$ her age. How many years ago was Zoe 4 times as old as her daughter?

5   Kaden had $10 less than Ben. When their mother gave both Kaden and Ben $4 each, Kaden had $\frac{7}{9}$ as much as Ben in the end. How much money did Kaden have at first?

6   There were 104 cookies in a box. The number of raisin cookies was $\frac{6}{7}$ the number of plain cookies. Chantalle ate an equal number of raisin and plain cookies. As a result, the ratio of the number of raisin cookies to the number of plain cookies left was 3 : 5. How many raisin cookies were left in the end?

7 There were 90 cookies in a box. The number of raisin cookies was $\frac{2}{3}$ the number of plain cookies. Chantalle ate an equal number of raisin and plain cookies. As a result, the ratio of the number of raisin cookies to the total number of cookies left was 1 : 5. How many cookies did Chantalle eat?

8 There were $\frac{3}{7}$ as many tables as chairs in a school hall. Mr. Chan added 60 tables and 60 chairs into the school hall for an event. As a result, the number of tables was $\frac{3}{5}$ the number of chairs. How many chairs were in the hall in the end?

9   Mark had 40% as much money as Joe at first. When each of them received $50 from their father, Mark had 60% as much as Joe. How much did Mark have in the end?

10 Michelle gave birth to her son when she was w years old. Find her son's age when she is 39 years old. Give your answer in terms of w.

Teacher's comment
Imagine W= #. Her son will be (39 – #) years old.

1 Kaden had $60. After he spent some money on a book and half of the remainder on a bag, he had $24 left. What was the cost of the book?

2   Jeremy had \$80. After he spent some money on a book and $\frac{1}{3}$ of the remainder on a bag, he had \$24 left. What was the cost of the book?

3 Kaden and Quan had $70 and $60 respectively at first. After Kaden spent $20 and Quan received some money from his mother, Quan had twice as much money as Kaden.

(a) How much did Kaden have in the end?

(b) How much did Quan receive from his mother?

> **Teacher's comment**
>
> Show in the model drawing that Quan had 2 times of what Kaden had in the end.

4 Ryan had $120 more than Kaden. Kaden had $\frac{1}{4}$ as much money as Ryan. Both of them spent a total of $170 on some gifts for their friends. As a result, Kaden had $\frac{2}{3}$ as much as Ryan.

(a) How much do they have altogether in the end?
(b) How much did Kaden have in the end?

5 Kaden had three times as much money as Quan. Quan had $15. After Kaden spent $10 and Quan received some money from his mother, Quan had $\frac{4}{5}$ as much money as Kaden.

(a) How much did Quan have in the end?
(b) How much did Quan receive from his mother?

6 Kaden had $\frac{2}{7}$ as much money as Quan. They had a total of $279 altogether. Their mother gave Kaden $138 and Quan some money. The ratio of Kaden's to Quan's money in the end was 4 : 7. How much did Quan receive from his mother?

Teacher's comment
Find out how much each person had at first.

7   Keith and Uri had a total of $80 at first. Keith received some money from his father and Uri spent $14 on a pencil case. Both of them had a total of $100 in the end. How much did Keith receive from his father?

8   There were 8,000 people at a concert hall at first. 40% of the people at the concert were men and the rest were women. After some men and 50 women left, the ratio of the number of men to women who remained in the concert hall was 3 : 5. How many people left the concert hall?

9   40% of the people at a concert were men and the rest were women. After some men and 24 women left, the ratio of the number of men to women who remained in the concert hall was 3 : 5. If there were 8,400 people at the concert hall in the end, how many people left the concert hall?

10 Jonas had $18. After buying 4 identical pens, he had $m left. What was the cost of one pen in terms of m?

> **Teacher's comment**
> If m = $6, we will take
> $18 – $6 = $12.
> Therefore, the cost of 4
> pens = $18 – m.

1   Kaden has 10 more stamps than Ron. How many stamps must Kaden give to Ron so that they will have the same number of stamps?

> **Teacher's comment**
>
> Cut the 10 stamps into 2 equal boxes in the model drawing.

2   Angela and Raul had some stickers. When Angela gave Raul 8 stickers, they had the same number of stickers in the end. How many more stickers did Angela have than Raul at first?

3   Kaden had 20 more stamps than Ron. Ron gave Kaden 1 stamp. How many more stamps did Kaden have than Ron in the end?

4   Lisa had 20 more apples than Joan. Lisa gave Joan 3 apples. How many more apples did Lisa have than Joan in the end?

5 Kaden had 20 more stamps than Ron. Kaden gave Ron 14 stamps. How many fewer stamps did Kaden have than Ron in the end?

> **Teacher's comment**
>
> Transfer parts of the model drawing from one person to another to compare the number of stamps each person had.

6   Nicole had 20 more cups than Isabel. Nicole gave Isabel 26 cups. How many fewer cups did Nicole have than Isabel in the end?

7 Teresa had 20 fewer cards than Sue. Sue gave Teresa a number of cards and, as a result, Teresa had 6 fewer cards than Sue. How many cards did Sue give Teresa?

8   Kaden and Ron had the same number of stamps. After Kaden gave 24 stamps to Ron, Ron had 4 times as many stamps as Kaden.

(a)   How many stamps did Kaden have in the end?

(b)   How many stamps did Ron have in the end?

9 Jessie had $80 less than Vincent at first. Vincent gave Jessie $60. The ratio of Jessie's money to Vincent's money now became 11 : 7. How much did Vincent have at first?

10 Jessie had $40 more than Vincent at first. Jessie gave $70 to Vincent. Jessie now had 20% as much as Vincent. How much money did Jessie have at first?

1   Janson bought 7 identical pens and had $1.20 left. He would need $1.40 more if he bought another 2 pens. Find the cost of 1 pen.

> **Teacher's comment**
> The remaining amount of money and the amount of money he needed will be the cost of 2 pens.

2 Janson bought 7 identical pens and had $4.20 left. If he had bought 12 identical pens and 4 identical erasers at $0.80 each, he would need $8.50 more. How much did Janson have at first?

3 Tom, Sam, and Amy had $320 altogether. Tom had $40 less than Sam. Sam had $90 more than Amy. How much did Amy have?

> **Teacher's comment**
>
> Compare the amounts of money Tom and Sam had and show that Amy had only one unit in the model drawing.

4   Tom and Sam had $62 altogether. Sam and Amy had $34 altogether. Tom had three times as much money as Amy.

   (a)   How much more did Tom have than Amy?
   (b)   How much did Tom have?

5 Remus bought a mug and 4 towels for $13. Joanne bought a mug and 7 towels for $19. Find the cost of the mug.

Teacher's comment

The difference in total cost is the cost of the extra towels.

6   There are 75 students in classes A and B altogether. There are 61 students in classes A and C altogether. The ratio of the number of students in Class B to Class C is 5 : 3. How many students are there in Class A?

7   Jane spent the same amount of money on 10 pencils and 14 erasers. Each pencil cost 20 cents more than each eraser. Find the cost of one eraser.

8   Logan bought 5 pens and 3 markers. Christopher bought 3 pens and 5 markers. Logan spent $0.90 more than Christopher. Find the price difference between 1 pen and 1 marker and state which item was more expensive.

9   Jane and Remus spent the same amount of money on some apples and pears. Jane bought 6 apples and 10 pears. Remus bought 14 apples and 5 pears. If Jane wanted to buy only apples, how many apples could she have bought with all her money?

10 Jessie had $17 more than Vincent at first. Vincent spent $9 less than Jessie at a sale. Vincent then had $\frac{7}{11}$ as much money as Jessie. How much did both of them have altogether in the end?

1 The width of a rectangle is $\frac{1}{4}$ its length. What is the length of the rectangle if its perimeter is 80 cm?

Teacher's comment
Add the units on all sides to find the perimeter.

2 The width of a rectangle is $\frac{2}{3}$ its length. Given that the perimeter of 2 such rectangles is 90 cm, find the width of the rectangle.

3 The length of a rectangle is $1\frac{1}{4}$ times its width. Given that the perimeter of the rectangle is 180 cm, find the area of the rectangle.

Teacher's comment
Find the length and the width of rectangle first before calculating the area.

4   The ratio of the length of a rectangle to its width is 4 : 3. Given that the perimeter of the rectangle is 70 cm, find the area of the rectangle.

5 The width of the rectangle is 50% its length. Given that the perimeter of 3 such rectangles is 90 cm, find the length of 1 rectangle.

6 The length of a rectangle is 250% its width. Given that the perimeter of the rectangle is 280 cm, find the width of the rectangle.

7   The length of a rectangle is 20% longer than its width. Given that the perimeter of the rectangle is 88 cm, find the length of the rectangle.

8 The length of a rectangle is 100% longer than its width. Given that the area of the rectangle is 98 cm², find the width of the rectangle.

9 Three identical circles were cut out from a rectangle cardboard with a perimeter of 80 cm. Find the circumference of 1 circle. (Take π as 3.14.)

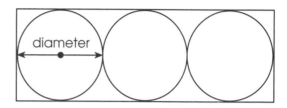

Teacher's comment

The circumference of a circle = π × diameter. The diameter of a circle is a straight line that cuts through the center of the circle with endpoints on the circle.

10 Eight identical circles were cut out from a 200 cm² rectangular cardboard. Find the perimeter of the rectangular cardboard.

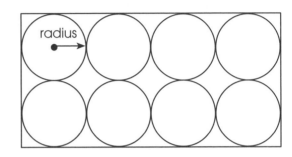

1 Irene bought 10 pens with $\frac{2}{5}$ of her money. If Irene were to buy another 24 pens, then she would need $18 more. Find the amount of money Irene had left after buying the 10 pens.

Teacher's comment
Find out how many pens she could buy if she had $18.

2 Willy bought 15 pears and Jack bought 18 oranges. They spent the same amount of money. The difference in cost between a pear and an orange was $0.10. How much did Willy spend on the 15 pears?

3 Ron puts all his nails into 2 large boxes and 6 small boxes. There are 20 more nails in one large box than one small box. The number of nails in the 2 large boxes was $\frac{1}{2}$ as many as the number of nails in the 6 small boxes. Find the number of nails in 1 large box.

> **Teacher's comment**
>
> Compare the number of nails in the two boxes by using the fraction given.

4 Andy and Marcus each bought the same storybook and both of them started reading their books on the same day. Marcus read 3 fewer pages than Andy each day. Marcus took 80 days to finish his storybook while Andy took 30 days fewer than him. Find the number of pages in the storybook.

5   Kaden, Amy, and John had an equal amount of money. Kaden bought 24 cards with all his money while John bought 30 stickers with all his money. Amy bought 8 cards and some stickers with all her money. How many stickers did Amy buy?

6   Ben had $\frac{1}{5}$ as many books as Jann. After Jann gave Ben 4 books, Ben had $\frac{1}{3}$ as many books as Jann. How many books did Jann have in the end?

7   The ratio of the number of apples Nicole and Hannah had was
        1 : 3. When Nicole bought 4 more apples and Hannah bought
        3 more apples, the ratio became 1 : 2. Find the number of apples
        Hannah had in the end.

8   The ratio of the number of magnets Nicole and Hannah had was 2 : 3. When Nicole bought 4 more magnets and Hannah bought 13 more magnets, the ratio became 1 : 2. Find the number of magnets Hannah had in the end.

9   Janet spent 30% of her money on 7 cupcakes and 4 cookies on Monday. The cost of each cupcake was twice the cost of each cookies. She bought some more cupcakes and another 10 cookies with $\frac{6}{7}$ of her remaining money on Tuesday. How many cupcakes did she buy on Tuesday?

10 The cost of a mango was 50% more than the cost of an apple. Sue used 25% of her money to buy 7 apples and 2 mangoes. How many more mangoes could Sue buy with 80% of her remaining money?

> **Teacher's comment**
> If she used 25% of her money, then 75% would be her remaining money.

1   4 years ago, the sum of Jeremy and Randy's age was 30. Find their total age now.

2 Kaden and Dave had an equal number of game cards at first. Kaden bought another 20 game cards and Dave bought another 47 game cards. How many more game cards did Dave have than Kaden in the end?

3   Kaden and Zoe had $30 and $50 respectively. How much more money must Kaden have so that he would have 4 times as much money as Zoe?

4 Christopher and Andy had 207 stamps. Christopher bought another 3 stamps and Andy lost 3 stamps. Find the total number of stamps they had in the end.

5 Kaden is 4 years old. Sally is 11 years old. What is their age difference? What is their age difference in 3 years?

6 Jonas had $18. After buying 4 identical pens, he had $10 left. What was the cost of one pen?

7   Kaden and Ron had the same number of stamps. If Kaden gave Ron 3 stamps, how many more stamps did Ron have than Kaden?

8 Janson bought 7 identical pens and had $4.20 left. He could have bought 10 pens with all his money. How much did Janson have?

9 The length of a rectangle is three times its width. What is the length of the rectangle if its perimeter is 72 cm?

10 2 jugs and 10 cups can hold 3,600 ml of water. Given that a cup can hold $\frac{1}{4}$ as much water as a jug, how much water can a jug hold? Give your answer in liters.

1 Sam had some money. He spent $\frac{3}{5}$ of his money. Sam's mother gave him $10. As a result, Sam had $38 in the end. How much did Sam spend?

2   Kelvin gave $\frac{2}{7}$ of his money to James. As a result, Kelvin had $140 and James had $100 in the end. How much did James have at first?

3 Kaden and Dan had a total of $240. Kaden gave $\frac{1}{5}$ of his money to Dan. As a result, both of them had the same amount of money in the end. How much did Dan have at first?

Teacher's comment
Kaden and Dan still had $240 altogether in the end.

4   Kaden and Dan had $200 altogether. Kaden gave $\frac{2}{7}$ of his money to Dan. As a result, Dan had 4 times as much money as Kaden. How much did Dan have at first?

5 Hector $\frac{1}{4}$ of his money and an additional $7 to Calista. He had $23 left. How much did Hector have at first?

6 Hector gave $\frac{1}{6}$ of his money to Calista. He spent $8 less than $\frac{1}{3}$ of his remaining money on a book. As a result, Hector had $68 left in the end. How much did Hector have at first?

> **Teacher's comment**
> Use model drawing to find out how much the remaining amount of money was.

7 Jenny gave $\frac{3}{8}$ of her money and an additional $13 to Lily. She spend another $\frac{3}{8}$ of her remaining money and had $45 left. How much did Jenny have at first?

> **Teacher's comment**
>
> $\frac{3}{8}$ of her money is not equal to $\frac{3}{8}$ of her remaining money.

8 Emma gave $\frac{2}{5}$ of her money and an additional $9 to Olivia. She gave $\frac{4}{7}$ of her remaining money and an additional $1 to Ava. Emma then had $17 left. How much did Emma have at first?

9 Hector gave $\frac{1}{4}$ of his money and an additional $1 to Calista. He gave $\frac{1}{5}$ of his remaining money and an additional $4 to Karen. The amount of money Hector had left in the end was $31 more than the amount of money he gave to Karen. Find the amount of money Hector gave to Calista.

10 Hector gave 40% of his money and an additional $5 to Calista. He gave 75% of his remaining money and an additional $6 to Karen. The amount of money Hector had left in the end was $44 less than the amount of money he gave to Karen. Find the amount of money Hector gave to Calista.

1   The difference between two digits is 4. What is the largest possible sum of the two digits?

> **Teacher's comment**
> The largest possible single-digit number is 9.

2 The average of four digits is 6. Two of the digits are 8 and 3. What is the largest difference between the other two digits?

3 The average of three 2-digit numbers is 61. One of the numbers is 33. What is the largest difference between the other two numbers?

> **Teacher's comment**
>
> What is the largest possible 2-digit number among the 3 numbers?

4   The average of three 2-digit numbers is 45. One of the numbers is 70. What is the largest difference between the other two numbers?

5 The average of three 2-digit odd numbers is 39. One of the numbers is 65. What is the largest difference between the other two numbers?

6   The average of three 2-digit even numbers is 80. One of the numbers is 76. What is the largest difference between the other two numbers?

7   The average of four 3-digit numbers is 500. Two of the numbers are 150 and 230. What is the largest difference between the other two numbers?

8 The average of four 3-digit odd numbers is 201. Two of the numbers are 301 and 203. What is the largest difference between the other two numbers?

9 There are two numbers A and B. A is a 2-digit number which is a multiple of 8. B is a 2-digit number which is a multiple of 20. What is the largest possible difference between the two numbers A and B?

Teacher's comment

A has to be the smallest number and B has to be the largest number possible in this question.

10   X is a 2-digit number. When X is divided by 5, it has a remainder of 2. Another 2-digit number, Y, when divided by 20, has a remainder of 3. What is the largest possible difference between the two numbers?

1   ABCD is a rectangular piece of paper. A corner of the paper was folded to form triangle GEF. Find ∠y.

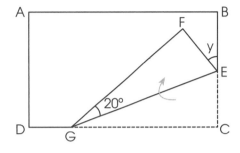

2   The figure on the right is drawn using straight lines only.
Find the value of $\angle m + \angle n + \angle o + \angle p + \angle q$.

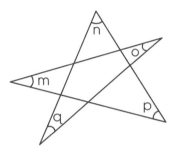

3   In the figure on the right, EFGH forms a square and EHI is an equilateral triangle. Find ∠IFH.

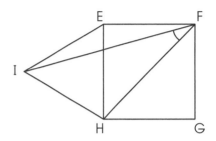

> **Teacher's comment**
> Make use of the isosceles triangle in the diagram to find the answer.

4   The figure below shows three identical squares. Find ∠x.

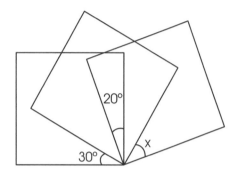

5 In the figure below, a rectangular piece of paper was folded as shown. Find ∠x.

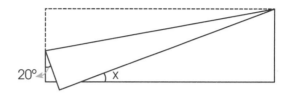

6 The corners of a cube, X, Y and Z, are joined together to form a triangle. What is ∠XYZ?

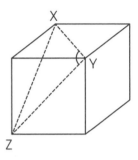

7   The figure below shows an equilateral triangular piece of paper folded along line FG, ∠EFH is 18°. Find ∠y.

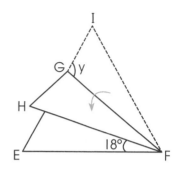

8 In the figure below, find the sum of ∠a, ∠b, ∠c, ∠d, ∠e, and ∠f.

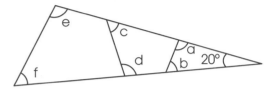

9 A rectangular piece of paper was folded as shown. Find ∠x.

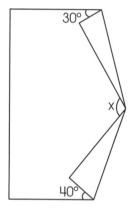

10 The figure on the right shows a 'star'. Find ∠x.

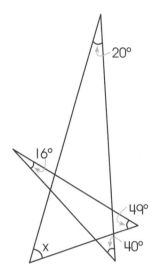

1 A muffin and a tart were sold at $3. Alice spent a total of $21 on the muffins and tarts. If she bought the same number of muffins and tarts, how many muffins and tarts in total did Alice buy?

2 Adam has the same number of twenty-cent coins and one-dollar coins. The total value of all the coins is $36. What is the total value of 1 twenty-cent coin and 1 one-dollar coin? Find the total number of coins Adam has.

3 A muffin cost $1.50 and a tart cost $1. Alice bought 2 more tarts than muffins. She spent a total of $14.50 on the muffins and tarts. How many muffins and tarts in total did Alice buy?

> **Teacher's comment**
>
> Consider putting a muffin and a tart as one set of food.

4 Ethan has one more twenty-cent coin than one-dollar coin. The total value of all the coins is $6.20. How many twenty-cent coins does Ethan have?

5   Lucas has 4 fewer one-dollar coins than ten-cent coins. The total value of all the coins is $7. How many coins does Lucas have in all?

6 Adam has a total of 40 coins. He has the same number of twenty-cent coins and one-dollar coins. Find the difference in value between the $1 coins and twenty-cent coins.

Teacher's comment
The difference between one $1 coin and one 20¢ coin is $0.80.

7   Adam has the same number of twenty-cent coins and one-dollar coins. The difference in value between all the twenty-cent coins and all the one-dollar coins is $7.20. How many coins does Adam have in all?

8   Jacob has 1 more twenty-cent coin than one-dollar coin. The total value of the one-dollar coins is $5.40 more than the total value of the twenty-cent coins. How many coins does Jacob have altogether?

9 Mason has three more $10 bills than $2 bills in his wallet. The total value of the $2 bills is $94 fewer than the total value of the $10 bills. How many $2 bills does Mason have?

10 Adam has three fewer one-dollar coins than ten-cent coins. The total value of the ten-cent coins is $7.80 less than the total value of the one-dollar coins. How many coins does Adam have in all?

1   Ramesh had some $2 bills and $5 bills in his wallet. There were 4 times as many $2 bills as $5 bills. Ramesh had $91 altogether. How many $2 bills did Ramesh have in total?

2 Ramesh has $\frac{1}{3}$ as many $2 bills as $5 bills. The total value of the $2 and $5 bills that Ramesh has is $136. How many $5 bills does Ramesh have?

Teacher's comment
Put one $2 bills and three $5 bills in one group.

3 $\frac{2}{5}$ of the fruits that Sue bought were oranges. The rest were apples. Each apple cost $0.50 and each orange cost $0.10 more. Sue spent a total of $10.80 on all the fruits. Find the number of apples Sue bought.

4 $\frac{2}{5}$ of the fruit that Sue bought were oranges. The rest were apples. Each apple cost $0.50 and each orange cost $0.10 more. Sue spent $1.80 less on all the oranges than all the apples. How many fruit did Sue buy altogether?

5 A football team played 38 games in a tournament and collected a total of 70 points. 3 points were awarded for a win and 1 point for games they tied. No points were deducted for games they lost. The team won twice as many games as they tied. Find the number of games the team lost.

6 Ken has a number of $2 bills, $5 bills, and $10 bills in his wallet. There are four times as many $2 bills as $5 bills. There are three times as many $5 bills as $10 bills. All the $2 bills and $10 bills in Ken's wallet add up to $306. How many $5 bills does Ken have in his wallet?

7   A piggy-bank has some 10-cent coins and one-dollar coins. The total value of the 10-cent coins is equal to the total value of the one-dollar coins. If there are 88 coins in all, how many 10-cent coins are there altogether?

> **Teacher's comment**
> How many 10-cent coins will make $1?

8 A pencil cost $\frac{2}{3}$ as much as an eraser. Tom bought a number of pencils and erasers. The total cost of all the pencils was 4 times as much as the total cost of all the erasers. Tom bought 35 pencils and erasers. How many pencils did Tom buy altogether?

9   Mr. Poh had some $10 bills, $5 bills, and $2 bills in his wallet. He had $159. $\frac{1}{5}$ of them were $10 bills, 3 fewer than $\frac{1}{2}$ of the remaining bills were $5 bills and the rest were $2 bills. How many $2 bills were there altogether?

Teacher's comment
Remove 3 $2 bills and add 3 $5 bills from the total number of bills.

10 There were 60 questions to be answered in a mathematical competition. The average number of questions answered correctly by all the participants was 44. The average number of questions answered correctly by the top 75% of the participants was 48. What was the average number of questions that were answered incorrectly by the bottom 25% of the participants?

1 Cookies are sold in packets of 3. Each packet of cookies cost $4. Owen needs at least 32 cookies. How much will Owen have to pay?

Teacher's comment
Owen will need to buy more cookies than he needs since they are sold in packets of 3.

2   Muffins are sold in packets of 3. Each packet of muffins cost $4. How many muffins can you buy with $25?

3 Cookies can only be sold in packets of 2. Each packet of cookies cost $3. How many cookies can you buy with $19?

4 Muffins can only be sold in packets of 3. Each packet of muffins cost $5. How many muffins can Owen buy with $22 and how much money he will have in the end after buying the muffins?

5 A customer gets one muffin free for every three muffins she buys. A muffin costs $1.50. May wants to buy 22 muffins. How much does she need?

6 A cupcake cost $1.30. A customer is entitled to buy one more cupcake at $1 after buying two cupcakes. Find the maximum number of cupcakes Owen can buy with $17.

7 An ice cream cone costs $1.60 each. Each customer is entitled to buy another two at a discount of $0.30 off the original price each after buying three. Find the maximum number of ice cream cones Owen can buy with $24 and the amount of money he will have in the end after buying the ice cream cones.

8 A substitute teacher will be paid $100 each day if he works from Monday to Friday. He will be paid $120 each day on Saturdays and Sundays. How many days will he have to work so that he can be paid $4,740 in total?

> **Teacher's comment**
> Find out the amount of money he will make in a week.

9   Connie started saving money in her piggy bank on a Wednesday.
She saved $0.50 each day. On which day of the week would she
have saved $23 in her piggy bank?

10 Connie started saving money in her piggy bank on a Friday. She saved $1 per day from Monday to Friday and $2 per day on Saturday and Sunday. On which day of the week would she have saved $32 in her piggy bank?

1 There were 9 street lamps at equal distance apart along a stretch of road. The distance between every 2 street lamps was 20 m. What was the distance from the first street lamp to the last street lamp?

Teacher's comment
How many spaces (gaps) are there between 9 street lamps?

2   12 pupils stood in a straight row at equal distances apart from each other. If the distance from the first to the last pupil was 66 m, what was the distance between one pupil and the next?

3 10 pupils were standing in a straight row at equal distances apart from each other. If the 2nd pupil was 20 m away from the 6th pupil, what was the distance between the first pupil and the last pupil?

4 Some pupils were standing in a straight row at equal distances apart from each other. The distance from the 3rd pupil and the 8th pupil was 10 m. If the distance from the first pupil to the last pupil was 30 m, how many pupils were there standing in the row altogether?

5   Mei placed some potted plants in a row from one end to the other end of the corridor. They were placed at an equal distance from one another. The distance between the 9th and the 13th potted plant was 24 m. If the length of the entire stretch of corridor was 78 m, find the total number of plants that were placed altogether.

6 Mr. Lim wanted to place some potted plants around a square garden. 1 potted plant was placed in each of the 4 corners. The rest of the plants were placed 5 m apart from one another along the 4 sides. If he placed 9 potted plants on one side of the square garden, find the perimeter of the square garden.

> **Teacher's comment**
> Find one length of the square garden.

7 Roads A and B were of the same length. Each of the 21 street lamps on Road A was 10 m apart. Road B had 4 fewer street lamps than Road A. Find the distance between 2 street lamps on Road B.

8 Two stretches of road were of the same length. There were 25 street lamps at equal distances on Road A. The distance between the 7th street lamp and the 11th street lamp was 80 m. Road B had 6 more street lamps than Road A. Find the distance between 2 street lamps on Road B if they were of an equal distance apart.

9 Dennis had 2 strings of the same length. Identical flags were tied to the first string at an equal spacing of 66 cm apart. A total of 36 flags were tied to the first string. The width of each flag was 20 cm. 8 more flags were tied to the second string. Find the spacing between 2 flags on the second string.

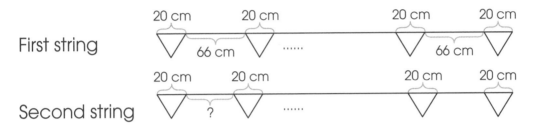

10 An elevator can travel from the 10th level to the 16th level in 3 s. If the distance between one level and the next is 2.5 m, what is the speed of the elevator?

Teacher's comment
Divide the distance travelled by the time taken to find the speed.

1 Bryan used $\frac{1}{7}$ of his savings to buy a book. He spent $\frac{1}{2}$ of the remaining money he had on a bag. What fraction of his savings was left?

2   Ling spent $\frac{1}{9}$ of her savings on a blouse and $\frac{1}{4}$ of the remainder on a bag. What fraction of her savings was left?

Teacher's comment
Show $\frac{1}{4}$ as the remaining units of the remainder in the model drawing.

3 Sofia spent $\frac{2}{3}$ of her savings on a blouse and $\frac{3}{4}$ of the remainder on a bag. What fraction of her savings was left?

4 Chloe spent $\frac{2}{5}$ of her savings on a blouse and $\frac{2}{3}$ of the remainder on a bag. What fraction of her savings was left?

5   Jason bought 5 kg of rice. He gave $\frac{3}{10}$ of the rice he bought to Connie. How many kilograms of rice did he give to Connie?

6 Alex and Belle had \$88. Alex saved $\frac{1}{3}$ of his money while Belle spent $\frac{4}{5}$ of her money. Given that Alex and Belle spent the same amount of money, how much did Alex save?

7 Alex had $57 less than Belle. Alex saved $\frac{3}{5}$ of his money while Belle spent $\frac{2}{3}$ of her money. Given that the amount Alex spent was $\frac{1}{4}$ of Belle's savings, how much did Belle spend?

Teacher's comment
Alex spent $\frac{2}{5}$ of his money and Belle saved $\frac{1}{3}$ of her money.

8 Alex had $28 more than Belle. Alex spent $\frac{3}{4}$ of his money while Belle spent $\frac{1}{9}$ of her money. Given that Alex's savings was $\frac{1}{2}$ as much as Belle's savings, find how much money Belle had at first.

9 Henry gave Zoe $420. He then spent $\frac{1}{4}$ of his remaining money on a bag. As a result, he had $\frac{6}{11}$ of his money left. How much money did Henry have at first?

10 Ryan had some blue and green buttons. $\frac{3}{7}$ of the buttons were blue and the rest were green. He gave away $\frac{2}{5}$ of his buttons. 80 of the buttons given away were blue. $\frac{2}{3}$ of the buttons left were green. How many buttons did Ryan have altogether at first?

1   Kaden and John had some marbles. John gave away $\frac{3}{5}$ as many marbles as Kaden and was left with 4 fewer marbles than the marbles he gave away. Kaden had $\frac{2}{5}$ as many marbles left as John. The difference between the number of marbles they had in the end was 21. How many marbles did Kaden have at first?

2 Kaden and John had 108 marbles altogether. Kaden gave away $\frac{1}{2}$ as many marbles as what John gave away. The number of marbles John had left was the same as the number of marbles he had given away. If John had $\frac{1}{2}$ as many marbles left as Kaden, how many marbles did John have at first?

3   The ratio of the number of marbles Kaden, Adam, and John gave away was 2 : 4 : 9. The number of marbles Kaden gave away was 2 fewer than the number of marbles he had left. Adam had $\frac{1}{2}$ as many marbles left as John. Kaden had $\frac{1}{2}$ as many marbles left as Adam. They had a total of 56 marbles left. How many marbles did John give away?

Teacher's comment
Form the ratio of the units of marbles they had left.

4 Leo and Isaac had 95 marbles altogether. Leo gave away 3 more marbles than Isaac. Isaac was left with 5 fewer than the marbles he gave away. Leo had 2 more marbles left than Isaac. How many marbles did Leo give away?

> **Teacher's comment**
>
> Draw a model by using the information in the question.

5   Kaden and John had 128 marbles altogether. Kaden gave away three times as many marbles as John. The marbles John had left was 4 fewer than the marbles he gave away. John had three times as many marbles left as Kaden. How many marbles did John have at first?

6 Caleb had 37 more marbles than David at first. Caleb gave away 4 times as many marbles as David. David was left with 5 more than the number of marbles he gave away. Caleb had twice as many marbles left as David. How many marbles did Caleb have in the end?

> **Teacher's comment**
>
> Let the number of marbles David gave away be 1 unit.

7 Leo had twice as many stickers as John at first. Leo gave away three times as many stickers as John. John was left with 10 fewer than the number of stickers he gave away. Leo had 15 stickers in the end. How many stickers did John have at first?

8 Kaden and John had 350 marbles altogether. Kaden gave away 25% as many marbles as John. John was left with 40 more than the number of marbles he gave away. Kaden had 25% as many marbles as John in the end. How many marbles did John have in the end?

9   Kaden and John had 300 marbles altogether. Kaden gave away 25% fewer marbles than John. John was left with 50% as many as the number of marbles he gave away. Kaden had 75% of the total number of marbles the boys left in the end. How many marbles did Kaden have in the end?

10 Liam had 75% more magnets than John at first. Liam gave away 200% as many magnets as John. John was left with 25% of the magnets he had at first. What fraction of Liam's magnets did he have in the end?

1 Mr. Poh and Mrs. Diaz had an equal number of stickers. Mr. Poh gave 8 stickers to each of his 15 students in Class A and did not have any sticker left. Mrs. Diaz gave each of her 12 students an equal number of stickers in Class B and did not have any stickers left. How many more stickers did each student in Class B get than each student in Class A?

> **Teacher's comment**
>
> Divide the difference between the total number of stickers left by the number of stickers each student received to find the number of students.

2   Mr. Ahmad has some stickers for his class. If he gave each student 3 stickers, then he would have 40 stickers left. If he gave each student 7 stickers, then he would have no stickers left. How many stickers did Mr. Ahmad have?

3 Mr. Poh bought some pencils for his class. If he gave each student 5 pencils, then he would need another 24 pencils. If he gave each student 3 pencils, then he would have no pencils left. How many pencils did Mr. Poh buy?

4   Mr. Lee had some stickers for his class. If he gave each student 7 stickers, then he would need another 5 stickers. If he gave each student 4 stickers, then he would have 40 stickers left. How many stickers did Mr. Lee have?

5   Mr. Kumar bought some stickers for his class. If he gave each student 7 stickers, then he would have 20 stickers left. If he gave each student 3 stickers, then he would have 140 stickers left. How many stickers did Mr. Kumar buy?

6 Mr. Johnson had some stamps for his class. If he gave each student 10 stamps, then he would need another 260 stamps. If he gave each student 4 stamps, then he would need another 20 stamps. How many stamps did Mr. Johnson have?

7   Mr. Poh had some pencils for his class. If he gave each student 7 pencils, then he would have 8 pencils left. If he gave each student 9 pencils, then the last 3 students would have only 5 pencils each. How many pencils did Mr. Poh have?

8   There were 27 equal rows of chairs in a hall. Yuri removed all the chairs in the last 4 rows and added them equally to the remaining rows. As a result, each row had 8 more chairs. How many chairs were there in the hall?

9 Connie, Ken, and Dan took a Mathematics test. Connie scored 3 marks above their average score. Ken scored 14 marks fewer than Connie. Find the difference between Dan's marks and Ken's marks.

10 Mark had x number of beads. John had 5 beads more than Mark. John had 4 beads more than Sam. What was the average number of beads the three boys had in terms of x?

Teacher's comment
If x = 10, John would have 10 + 5 = 15. Therefore, John had (x + 5) beads.

1   Jessie had some money at first. She spent $17 on a book. Her mother then gave her $20. Jessie also spent $3 on a cupcake. As a result, she had $28 left in her purse. How much did Jessie have at first?

2 The average of three digits is 5. One of the digits is 4. What is the largest difference between the other two digits?

3 ABCD is a square piece of paper. A corner of the paper was folded to form triangle EFG. Find ∠y.

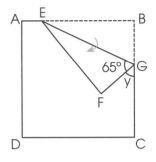

4   Adam has a total of 40 coins. He has the same number of twenty-cent coins and one-dollar coins. He arranges 1 twenty-cent coin and 1 one-dollar coin into 1 pair. What is the value of 1 pair of coins? How much does Adam have?

5 Ramesh had some $2 bills and $5 bills in his wallet. He had a $5 bill for every three $2 bills. Given that he had a total of $99, how many $2 bills did Ramesh have in total?

6 Cookies are sold in packets of 4. Owen needs at least 21 cookies. How many packets will Owen have to buy?

7   5 pupils are standing in a straight row at 3 m apart from each other. What is the distance from the first pupil to the last pupil?

8   Bryan had a total of $180. He used $\frac{1}{6}$ of his savings on a meal in a restaurant. He spent $\frac{2}{3}$ of the remaining money he had on a badminton racket. What was the cost of the badminton racket?

9   Kaden and John had some marbles. Kaden gave away 18 marbles and John gave away $\frac{1}{3}$ as many marbles as Kaden. John had 2 more marbles left than the marbles he gave away. Kaden had twice as many marbles left as John. How many marbles did Kaden and John have in total at first?

10   Mr. Poh had some stickers for his class of 14 students. If he gave each student 3 stickers, then he would have 39 stickers left. If he gave each student 5 stickers, then how many stickers would Mr. Poh have left?

1 Nelson paid $60 for a shirt after a discount of 20%. What was the price of the shirt before the discount?

2   Terence spent 20% of his savings on a watch and 30% of the remainder on a wallet. He had $840 left. What was the amount of money Terence had at first?

> **Teacher's comment**
>
> The amount of savings is not the same as the total amount of the remainder.

3   Judy baked some muffins. She gave away 20% of her muffins to her colleagues and 50% of the remaining muffins to her relatives. What percentage of her muffins did she give away altogether?

4 30% of the people in a hall were children. 20% of the children were boys. What percentage of the people were girls?

5 Sam lost 20% of his money and spent 20% of his remaining money. What percentage of his money was left in the end?

6 Joseph, Devi, and Luke received some money from their parents. Joseph had 60% as much money as the total amount Devi and Luke had. After spending 80% of his money, Joseph had $114 left. Find the total amount of money the three children had at first.

7   10% of the spectators in a stadium are children. 30% of the remainder are women. 60% of the children are boys. What is the ratio of men to girls?

8 Jessie had 20% less money than Minna. Charles had 15% more money than Jessie. If Charles had $184, how much did Minna have?

9 The entrance fee to the zoo for each person is $27 after a discount of 10%. Children below 10 years old are given a further $9 discount. What is the total percentage discount given to children below 10 years old for the entrance fee to the zoo?

10 Connie paid $27 for a belt after a discount at a bazaar. She then bought a skirt from another shop. She spent a total of $72 on these two items altogether. She paid 40% less for the belt than the skirt. She saved $12. Given that Connie was given a 10% discount on the belt, find the percentage discount given for the skirt. Round off your answer to one decimal place if necessary.

1 There are 5% fewer girls than boys in a badminton club. Given that there are 4 more boys than girls, find the total number of members in the club.

> **Teacher's comment**
> Let the total number of boys be 100%.

2   Christie spent 80% more than the amount she saved in a typical month. Given that she spent $63 for the month, find the allowance she had at the start of each month.

> **Teacher's comment**
> Let the amount she saved by 100%.

3 The width of a rectangle is 60% shorter than the length of a rectangle. Given that the perimeter of the rectangle is 140 cm, find the width of the rectangle.

4   Class X has 50% more students than Class Y. Class X has 40% fewer students than Class Z. Given that there are 80 students in the 3 classes, how many students are there in Class X?

5   Class A has 50% more students than Class B. Class B has 50% more students than Class C. What is the ratio of the number of students in Class A to Class C?

6   Class A has 25% fewer students than Class B. Class A has 6 more students than Class C. If there are 104 students in the 3 classes, how many students are there in Class C?

7   45% of the students in a class are boys. The number of girls who wear glasses is 20% more than the number of girls who do not wear glasses. What is the percentage of the girls who wear glasses in the class?

> **Teacher's comment**
> Compare the girls who wear and do not wear glasses with a ratio.

8   There were 42 students in the classroom. There were 10% more girls than boys. A few girls went to the restroom. As a result, the number of boys became 25% more than the number of girls in the classroom. How many girls went to the restroom?

9 The usual price of a book is 25% more than the discounted price. What percentage of the usual price of the book is the discount?

10 Ben drove for 15 minutes at an average speed of 50 km/h at first. He then drove another 6 km at an average speed that was 44% more than his earlier speed. What was his average speed for the whole journey?

Teacher's comment
Multiply the time taken with speed to find the distance he travelled. $\left(15 \text{ minutes} = \dfrac{1}{4} \text{ hour}\right)$

1 What was the percentage increase in the number of cars sold from March to May?

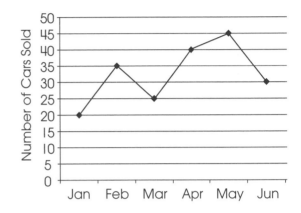

2   In a school, there were 20 male teachers and 60 female teachers. 3 male teachers left the school and 7 female teachers joined the school. Find the percentage increase in the number of teachers in the school.

Teacher's comment
Let the initial total number of teachers be 100%.

3 Ivy, Ken, and Ron shared some sweets in the ratio 5 : 4 : 2. Ken gave some of his sweets to Ivy and Ron. As a result, his sweets decreased by 75%. After receiving some sweets from Ken, Ron's sweets increased by 50%. Find the percentage increase in the number of sweets that Ivy had.

4 In a school, there were 112 male and female teachers. More female teachers joined the school and as a result, the number of female teachers increased by 20%. 5 male teachers left the school. There were 123 teachers in the end. Find the total number of male teachers at first.

5 Judy was given a fixed amount of salary each month. In November, she saved $1,000 and spent the rest. In December, she saved 20% more and her expenditure decreased by 5%. What was Judy's monthly salary?

6 Cheryl earned a fixed income each month. In September, Cheryl spent some money and saved the rest. In October, the amount she spent increased by 20% and she saved 40% less compared to the previous month. What fraction of Cheryl's income in September did she spend?

7   Siti's monthly allowance increased by 5% in every subsequent month. If her allowance in March was $40, find her monthly allowance in May.

> **Teacher's comment**
> The total percentage for each month is always 100%.

8 Ray scored 75 marks for his first math test. His math score increased by 20% on his second math test. However, for his third math test, his math score decreased by 20%. What was his math score for his third math test?

9 Jason had 40% fewer coins than Tom. Jason gave his sister some of his coins. As a result, the number of coins he had decreased by 25%. How many coins did Jason have left in the end if both of them had 58 coins altogether in the end?

10   If the length of a square decreased by 20%, find the percentage decrease in the area of the square.

1 The volume of a cube is 125 cm³. Find the length of the edge of the cube.

> **Teacher's comment**
> Count and find out what number when multiplied by 3 will give you 125.

2   The base area of a cube is 9 cm². Find the volume of the cube.

3 The total surface area of a cube is 294 cm². Find the volume of the cube.

> **Teacher's comment**
> A cube has 6 surfaces.

4   The volume of a cube is 729 cm³. Find the total surface area of the cube.

5   The volume of a cube is 1,000 cm³. Find the total length of all the edges of the cube.

6 The total length of all the edges of a cube is 96 cm. Find the volume of the cube.

7   The length of Cube X is 2 times the length of Cube Y. The volume of Cube Y is 27 cm³. What is the volume of Cube X?

8 The length of Cube P is $\frac{1}{4}$ the length of Cube Q. The volume of Cube Q is 512 cm³. Find the total volume of the two cubes.

9   The length of Cube J is 75% the length of Cube K. The volume of Cube J is 216 cm³. Find the volume of Cube K.

10 The ratio of the length of Cube Y to Cube Z is 3 : 1. Find the ratio of the volume of Cube Y to Cube Z.

1   Kelly takes 3 hours to clean a fish tank. Richard takes 6 hours to clean an identical fish tank. If they are to clean the fish tank together, what fraction of the fish tank can they clean in an hour?

> **Teacher's comment**
>
> Find the fraction of the fish tank each person can clean in one hour.

2   Kelly takes 4 hours to clean a fish tank. Richard takes 6 hours to clean an identical fish tank. If they are to clean the fish tank together, what fraction of the fish tank can they clean in an hour?

3 James took 4 hours to clean a fridge. Bryan took 12 hours to clean an identical fridge. If both of them worked together, how long would they need to clean the fridge?

4   Kelly takes 75 minutes to clean a set of windows by herself and Richard takes 50 minutes to clean the same set of windows. Find the time taken for both of them to clean the windows together.

5   Kelly took 4 hours to paint a room. Richard took 8 hours to paint an identical room. If both of them worked together, how long would they take to paint the room?

6 Emily took 6 hours to clean a cabinet. Jack and Emily took 2 hours to clean the same cabinet if they worked together. How long would Jack take to clean the cabinet by himself?

7   Jackson jogged from point A to point B at a speed of 200 m/min and Gary jogged from point B to point A at a speed 10 m/min slower than Jackson's speed. Both of them started jogging at the same time and did not change their speeds throughout the journey. When Jackson reached point A, Gary was still 120 m away from point B. What was the distance between point A and point B?

Teacher's comment
The speed difference caused the difference in the distance travelled by both boys.

8   Jack and Gary started jogging from point A to point B at the same time. When Jack reached point B in 2 hours, Gary had only completed 90% of the journey. Given than the speed difference between Jack and Gary was 0.8 km/h, find the distance from point A to point B.

Teacher's comment
Since the speed difference is 0.8 km/h, 0.8 km × 2 = 1.6 km. They are 1.6 km apart after 2 hours.

9 Jack and Gary started jogging from the same spot in opposite directions along a straight path. Both of them jogged for $\frac{3}{4}$ h. They were 15 km apart in the end. Given that Jack's average speed was 12 km/h, what was Gary's average speed in km/h?

Teacher's comment
Take speed × time to find the distance Jack travelled first.

10 Jackson and Mary started jogging from the same spot in the same direction along a jogging track. They jogged for 20 minutes. Jackson was 350 m ahead of Mary when he reached the finishing line. Find their speed difference. Leave your answer in km/h.

Teacher's comment
350 m was the distance they were apart since they travelled at different speeds.

1   Find the average of numbers 1 to 20.

2   What is the sum of numbers 10 to 40?

3   What is the average of the even numbers from 20 to 52?

> **Teacher's comment**
> Find out the number of
> even numbers from
> 20 – 52.

4   The average of 3 consecutive even numbers is 50. What is the largest of the 3 numbers?

5 The sum of twenty-one consecutive whole numbers is 735. Find the smallest number.

6 What is the difference between the sum of odd numbers and the sum of even numbers from 1 to 50?

> **Teacher's comment**
> The difference between two consecutive numbers is always 1.

7   What is the sum of $\frac{1}{4} + \frac{2}{4} + \frac{3}{4} + 1 + 1\frac{1}{4} + \ldots + 9\frac{1}{4} + 9\frac{2}{4} + 9\frac{3}{4} + 10$?

8   What is the sum of $0.1 + 0.2 + 0.3 + \ldots + 19.7 + 19.8 + 19.9$?

9   What is the sum of 1 + 1 + 1 + 2 + 2 + 2 + 3 + 3 + 3 + ... + 15 + 15 + 15?

10 Given that the average of some consecutive numbers adding from 1 is 25, find the sum of the consecutive numbers.

> **Teacher's comment**
>
> The average of a sum of number is always the number in the middle.

1 $\frac{2}{5}$ of Amy's money was $\frac{3}{4}$ of Ben's money. When Ben gave Amy $28, both of them would have the same amount of money. How much did Amy have at first?

Teacher's comment
Multiply the fractions and make the numerators of both fractions the same number.

2 $\frac{4}{5}$ of Amy's money was $\frac{2}{7}$ of Ben's money. When Ben spent $20 on a book, he would still have $16 more than Amy. How much did Amy have at first?

3 $\frac{2}{5}$ of Ella's money was $\frac{6}{7}$ of Noah's money. After Noah received $20 from his mother and Ella spent $36 on a bag, both of them had an equal amount of money left. How much did Ella have in the end?

4 $\frac{1}{2}$ of Amy's money was equal to $\frac{3}{4}$ of Ben's money. If Amy gave Ben $5, then he would have $6 less than Amy. How much did Ben have at first?

5 $\frac{3}{5}$ of Amy's money was $\frac{4}{5}$ of Ben's money. If Ben gave Amy $30, then she would have $100 more than the amount he had left. How much did Ben have at first?

6 $\frac{1}{3}$ of Mia's money was $\frac{4}{5}$ of Alan's money. If Mia gave $18 to Alan and he returned $4 to her a few days later, then both of them would have an equal amount of money left. How much did Mia have at first?

> **Teacher's comment**
>
> Find how much more money Amy had than Ben.

7 $\frac{3}{5}$ of Amy's money was twice as much as $\frac{1}{4}$ of Ben's money. If Amy gave Ben $3, then he would have $26 more than the amount she had left. How much did Ben have at first?

8 $\frac{1}{5}$ of Amy's money was $12 more than $\frac{1}{3}$ of Ben's money. When Amy gave Ben $50, both of them had the same amount of money in the end. How much did Amy have at first?

9 $\frac{2}{5}$ of Zoe's money was $12 more than $\frac{2}{3}$ of Luke's money. When Zoe gave Luke $50, both of them had the same amount of money in the end. How much did Luke have at first?

10 Amy and Ben had the same amount of money at first. When Amy gave Ben $36, 50% of the amount of money Amy had left was the same as 75% of what Ben had left. How much did they have in total at first?

1   One person can sit at each side of a square table as shown in the diagram below.

   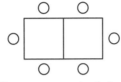   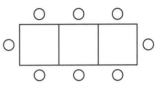

I square table   2 square tables   3 square tables

(a) If 10 square tables are joined end to end to form a long table, how many people can be seated at the long table?

(b) How many tables are needed to seat 40 people?

2 Kelly wants to form a square with rectangular cards each measuring 12 cm by 10 cm. How many such rectangular cards must she use to make the smallest possible square?

10 cm

12 cm

3   The area of the shaded part of square ABCD shown below is 51 cm². What is the area of square ABCD?

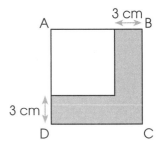

4 A wheel with diameter of 21 cm completed 10 revolutions as it rolled from wall X to wall Y. What was the distance between the two walls? $\left(\text{Take } \pi = \frac{22}{7}\right)$

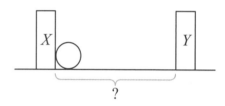

Teacher's comment

Find the circumference of 10 revolutions and add 2 radii to find the distance between the walls.

5   6 teams participated in a soccer tournament. Each team played once against each of the other teams. How many games were played in total?

6 In the figure shown below, EFGH is a rectangle and GHI is a triangle. The shaded area A is 48 cm² more than the shaded area B. What is the perimeter of rectangle EFGH?

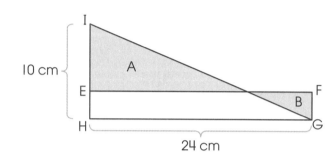

Teacher's comment

Find the area of rectangle first.

7   In the figure shown below, QRUV is a square. Line QS is 15 cm and line WU is 35 cm. What is the perimeter of rectangle PSTW?

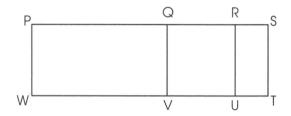

8 The figure below shows 3 overlapping identical triangles. The area of each equal triangle is 60 cm² and the area of the figure is 160 cm². What is the area of the shaded part of the figure?

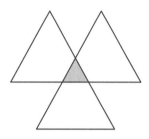

9 The figure below shows a rectangle ABCD with 4 squares around it. The perimeter of rectangle ABCD is 30 cm and the total area of the squares is 306 cm². Find the area of ABCD.

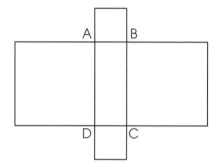

10 Figures A and B are two similar rectangular containers filled with the same amount of water and 7 identical blocks. Figure A has a base area of 350 cm². What is the volume of one of the blocks in the container?

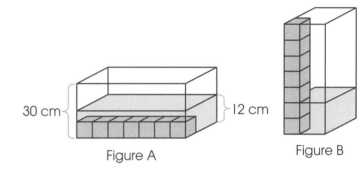

Figure A

Figure B

Chapter 1 Before and After – Adjusting

1 All are older by 6 years now.
Increase in total age (4 people) → 6 × 4 = 24
Total age now → 20 + 24 = 44
Their total age is **44** years.

2 All were 4 years younger then.
Decrease in total age (3 people) → 4 × 3 = 12
Total age 4 years ago → 38 − 12 = 26
Their total age was **26** years.

3 Difference in total age → 40 − 30 = 10
Difference in the total age comes from both of them equally.
Age difference for each person → 10 ÷ 2 = 5
In **5** years, their total age will be 40 years.

4 Difference in total age → 2 × 6 = 12
Total age now → 18 + 12 = 30

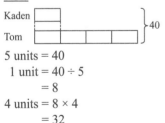

3 units = 30
 1 unit = 30 ÷ 3
    = 10
2 units = 10 × 2
    = 20
Jeremy is **20** years old now.

5 Total age now → 54 − 7 − 7 = 40
Now

Kaden
Tom
}40

5 units = 40
 1 unit = 40 ÷ 5
    = 8
4 units = 8 × 4
    = 32
Tom is **32** years old now.

6 Total age 10 years ago → 102 − 10 − 10 − 10 = 72
10 years ago

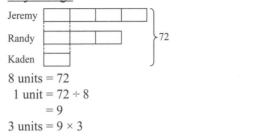

8 units = 72
 1 unit = 72 ÷ 8
    = 9
3 units = 9 × 3
    = 27
Randy's age now → 27 + 10 = 37
Randy is **37** years old now.

7 (a) Total number of marbles in the end → 46 + 10
                          = 56
After

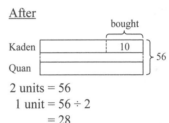

2 units = 56
 1 unit = 56 ÷ 2
    = 28
Kaden had **28** marbles in the end.

(b) Number of marbles Kaden had at first
    → 28 − 10
    = 18
Kaden had **18** marbles at first.

8 Total number of marbles in the end → $81 - 11 + 6$
$$= 76$$

After

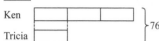

| Ken | | | |
| Tricia | | | |

76

$4 \text{ units} = 76$
$\quad 1 \text{ unit} = 76 \div 4$
$\qquad\quad = 19$
$3 \text{ units} = 19 \times 3$
$\qquad\quad = 57$

Before

lost

| Ken | 19 | 19 | 19 | 11 |

57 remaining

Number of marbles Ken had at first → $57 + 11$
$$= 68$$

Ken had **68** marbles at first.

---

9 Before

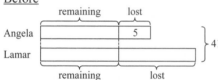

remaining lost

| Angela | | 5 | |
| Lamar | | | |

41

remaining lost

$41 - 5 = 36$
$3 \text{ units} = 36$
$\quad 1 \text{ unit} = 36 \div 3$
$\qquad\quad = 12$
$2 \text{ units} = 12 \times 2$
$\qquad\quad = 24$

Lamar had **24** stickers at first.

---

10 $1 - \dfrac{2}{5} = \dfrac{3}{5}$

Gabriel after buying 16 toy cars

James at first

$40 + 16$

$\frac{3}{5}$ remaining $\frac{2}{5}$ lost

$40 + 16 = 56$
$8 \text{ units} = 56$
$\quad 1 \text{ unit} = 56 \div 8$
$\qquad\quad = 7$
$3 \text{ units} = 7 \times 3$
$\qquad\quad = 21$

Number of toy cars Gabriel had at first → $21 - 16$
$$= 5$$

Gabriel had **5** toy cars at first.

Chapter 2 Before and After – Comparing

1 Before

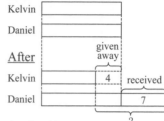

| Kelvin | | |
| Daniel | | |

given away

After

| Kelvin | | 4 | received |
| Daniel | | | 7 |

?

$4 + 7 = 11$
Daniel had **11** more erasers than Kelvin in the end.

---

2 Before

| Kaden | | |
| Dave | | |

After

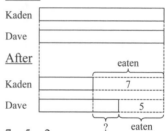

eaten

| Kaden | | 7 | |
| Dave | | | 5 |

? eaten

$7 - 5 = 2$
Dave had **2** more cookies than Kaden in the end.

---

3 (a) Before

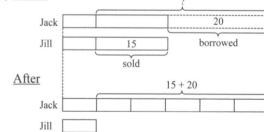

?

| Jack | | | 20 |
| Jill | | 15 | borrowed |

sold

After

$15 + 20$

| Jack | | | | | |
| Jill | | |

$15 + 20 = 35$
Jack had **35** more books than Jill in the end.

(b) $5 \text{ units} = 35$
$\quad 1 \text{ unit} = 35 \div 5$
$\qquad\quad = 7$
$6 \text{ units} = 7 \times 6$
$\qquad\quad = 42$

Jack had **42** books in the end.

---

4   Before

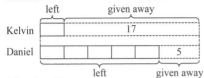

17 − 5 = 12
4 units = 12
 1 unit = 12 ÷ 4
    = 3
5 units = 3 × 5
    = 15
15 + 5 = 20
Daniel had **20** paper clips at first.

5   Before

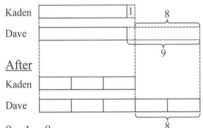

9 − 1 = 8
2 units = 8
 1 unit = 8 ÷ 2
    = 4
8 units = 4 × 8
    = 32
Total stamps Kaden and Dave bought → 32 − 1 − 9
                    = 22
Kaden and Dave bought **22** stamps altogether.

6

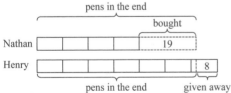

19 + 8 = 27
3 units = 27
 1 unit = 27 ÷ 3
    = 9
4 units = 9 × 4
    = 36
Nathan had **36** pens at first.

7   (a) Before

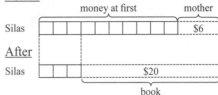

$20 − $6 = $14
Difference in the amount of money Silas had at first and in the end was **$14**.

(b) 7 units = 14
   1 unit = 14 ÷ 7
      = 2
  10 units = 2 × 10
      = 20
  Silas had **$20** at first.

8   Before

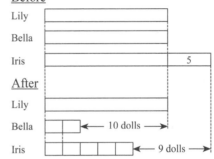

10 + 5 − 9 = 6
3 units = 6
 1 unit = 6 ÷ 3
    = 2
2 units = 2 × 2
    = 4
4 + 10 = 14
Lily had **14** dolls.

9 <u>Before</u>

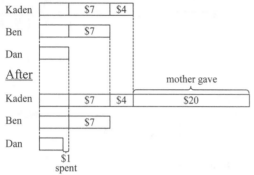

<u>After</u>

mother gave

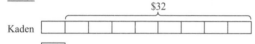

Difference in amount of money Kaden and Dan had in the end → $1 + $7 + $4 + $20
        = $32

<u>After</u>

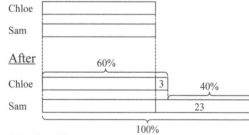

8 units = 32
  1 unit = 32 ÷ 8
       = 4
9 units = 4 × 9
       = 36
$36 − $20 = $16
Kaden had **$16** at first.

10 <u>Before</u>

Chloe

Sam

<u>After</u>

60%

Chloe   3
        40%
Sam   23

100%

23 − 3 = 20
Sam had 20 more apples than Chloe in the end.
100% − 60% = 40%
  40% → 20
  10% → 20 ÷ 4 = 5
100% → 5 × 10 = 50
50 − 23 = 27
Sam had **27** apples at first.

Chapter 3   Before and After – One Quantity Unchanged

1 <u>Before</u>

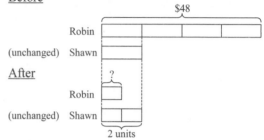

$48

Robin

(unchanged)   Shawn

<u>After</u>

?

Robin

(unchanged)   Shawn

2 units

Shawn's money (unchanged) → $48 ÷ 4 = $12
2 units = 12
  1 unit = 12 ÷ 2
       = 6
1 unit in the after model → $6
Robin had **$6** in the end.

2 <u>Before</u>

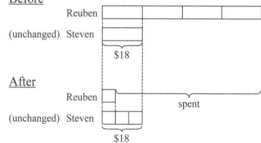

Reuben

(unchanged)   Steven

$18

<u>After</u>

Reuben

spent

(unchanged)   Steven

$18

Reuben's money at first → $18 × 4 = $72
Reuben's money in the end → $18 ÷ 3 = $6
Reuben spent → $72 − $6 = $66
Reuben spent **$66**.

3 <u>Before</u>

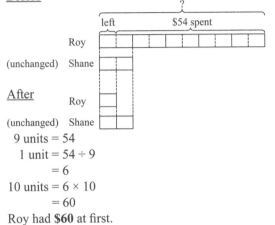

9 units = 54
  1 unit = 54 ÷ 9
        = 6
10 units = 6 × 10
        = 60
Roy had **$60** at first.

4 <u>Before</u>

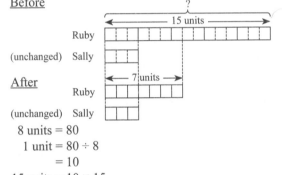

8 units = 80
  1 unit = 80 ÷ 8
        = 10
15 units = 10 × 15
        = 150
Ruby had **$150** at first.

5 <u>Before</u>

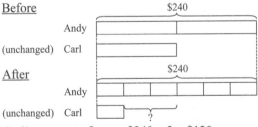

Carl's money at first → $240 ÷ 2 = $120
Carl's money in the end → $240 ÷ 6 = $40
Amount Carl spent → $120 − $40 = $80
Carl spent **$80**.

6 <u>Before</u>

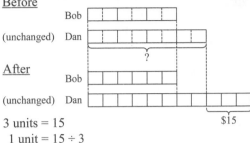

3 units = 15
  1 unit = 15 ÷ 3
        = 5
8 units = 5 × 8
        = 40
Dan had **$40** at first.

7 <u>Before</u>

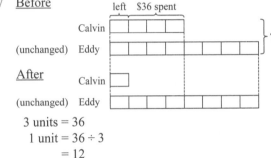

3 units = 36
  1 unit = 36 ÷ 3
        = 12
12 units = 12 × 12
        = 144
Both of them had **$144** altogether at first.

8 <u>Before</u>

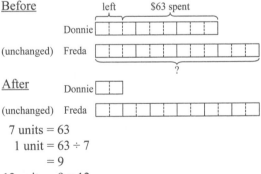

7 units = 63
  1 unit = 63 ÷ 7
        = 9
12 units = 9 × 12
        = 108
Freda had **$108**.

9 Before

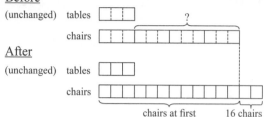

(unchanged) tables

chairs

After

(unchanged) tables

chairs

chairs at first   16 chairs bought

2 units = 16

1 unit = 16 ÷ 2

    = 8

9 units = 8 × 9

    = 72

There were **72** more chairs than tables at the café at first.

---

10 $20\% = \frac{1}{5}$

Before

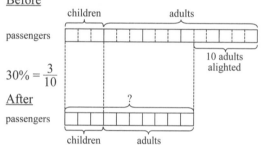

children   adults

passengers

$30\% = \frac{3}{10}$

10 adults alighted

After

passengers

?

children   adults

5 units = 10

1 unit = 10 ÷ 5

    = 2

10 units = 2 × 10

     = 20

20 passengers were on the bus in the end.

Chapter 4   Before and After – Total Unchanged

1 (a) After

Christopher

Andy

} 200

Total number of stamps in the end

→ 200 + 21 − 21

  = 200

They had **200** stamps altogether in the end.

(b) 200 ÷ 2 = 100

They each had 100 stamps in the end.

100 + 21 = 121

Andy had **121** stamps at first.

---

2 After

Christopher

Andy   10

} 300

?   given by Christopher

6 units = 300

1 unit = 300 ÷ 6

    = 50

Andy has 50 stamps in the end.

50 − 10 = 40

Andy had **40** stamps at first.

---

3 Total number of stamps in the end

→ 207 + 12 − 12

  = 207

After

Christopher

Andy

} 207

3 units = 207

1 unit = 207 ÷ 3

    = 69

2 units = 69 × 2

    = 138

Andy had 138 stamps in the end.

138 + 12 = 150

Andy had **150** stamps at first.

---

4 (a) <u>Before</u>

3 units = 60
  1 unit = 60 ÷ 3
        = 20
2 units = 20 × 2
        = 40
Alice had 40 apples at first.
Don had **20** apples at first.

(b) <u>After</u>

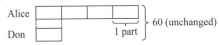

5 parts = 60
  1 part = 60 ÷ 5
        = 12
Don had 12 apples in the end.
20 − 12 = 8
Don gave Alice **8** apples.

5 <u>Before</u>

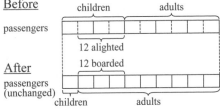

3 units = 12
  1 unit = 12 ÷ 3
        = 4
6 units = 4 × 6
        = 24
There were **24** adults on the bus at first.

6 <u>Before</u>

<u>After</u>

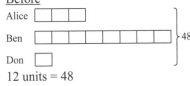

2 units = 10
  1 unit = 10 ÷ 2
        = 5
6 units = 5 × 6
        = 30
Alice had **30** apples at first.

7 <u>Before</u>

12 units = 48
   1 unit = 48 ÷ 12
         = 4

<u>After</u>

Alice
Ben   } 48
Don

48 ÷ 3 = 16
16 − 4 = 12
Don received **12** apples from Ben.

8 Before

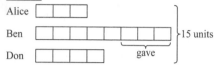

After

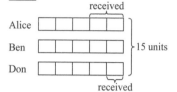

Each would have 5 units of apples in the end.
3 units = 21
  1 unit = 21 ÷ 3
      = 7
8 units = 7 × 8
      = 56
Ben had **56** apples at first.

---

9 Before

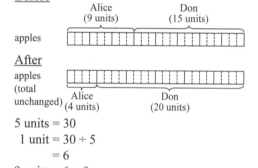

After
apples
(total unchanged)

5 units = 30
  1 unit = 30 ÷ 5
      = 6
9 units = 6 × 9
      = 54
Alice had **54** apples at first.

---

10 Before

marbles

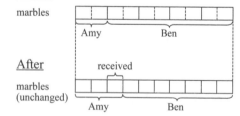

After

marbles
(unchanged)

Ben had 8 units at first.
He gave 1 unit to Amy.
Ben gave $\frac{1}{8}$ of the marbles he had at first to Amy.

Chapter 5   Before and After – Difference Unchanged

1 Before

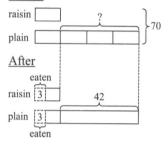

After
eaten

5 units = 70
  1 unit = 70 ÷ 5
      = 14
3 units = 14 × 3
      = 42

There are **42** more plain cookies than raisin cookies in the end and beginning.

---

2 Before

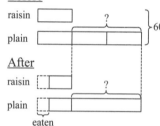

After

4 units = 60
  1 unit = 60 ÷ 4
      = 15
2 units = 15 × 2
      = 30

There were **30** more plain cookies than raisin cookies in the end.

Grade 5+
Singapore Math Challenge Word Problems

3   Now

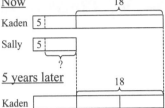

Kaden 5

Sally 5
             ?

5 years later

Kaden

Sally

2 units = 18
  1 unit = 18 ÷ 2
        = 9
In five years Sally is 9 years old.
9 − 5 = 4
Sally is **4** years old now.

4   Now

$\frac{1}{3} \times 36 = 12$

The daughter is 12 years old.
Age difference = 36 − 12
                      = 24

Zoe

daughter   24

24 ÷ 3 = 8
12 − 8 = 4
Zoe was 4 times her daughter's age **4** years ago.

5   Before

Kaden $4 $10

Ben $4

After

Kaden $10

Ben

2 units = 10
  1 unit = 10 ÷ 2
        = 5
7 units = 5 × 7
        = 35
$35 − $4 = $31
Kaden had **$31** at first.

6   Before

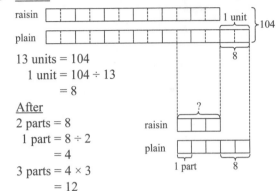

raisin   1 unit
                                  104
plain
                                  8

13 units = 104
  1 unit = 104 ÷ 13
        = 8
After
2 parts = 8
  1 part = 8 ÷ 2
        = 4
3 parts = 4 × 3
        = 12

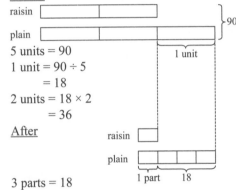

12 raisin cookies were left in the end.

7   Before

raisin
                                  90
plain
                          1 unit

5 units = 90
1 unit = 90 ÷ 5
      = 18
2 units = 18 × 2
        = 36
After   raisin

                 plain
                      1 part   18

3 parts = 18
  1 part = 18 ÷ 3
        = 6
36 − 6 = 30 (Raisin cookies eaten)
2 × 30 = 60
Chantalle ate **60** cookies.

8   Before

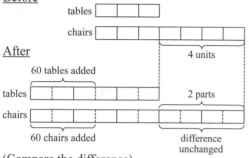

(Compare the difference)
 2 parts = 4 units
 1 part = 2 units
 5 parts = 2 × 5
       = 10 units
 3 units = 60
 1 unit = 60 ÷ 3
       = 20
 10 units = 20 × 10
        = 200
There were **200** chairs in the hall in the end.

9   Before
40% = $\frac{2}{5}$

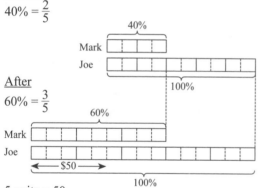

After
60% = $\frac{3}{5}$

5 units = 50
 1 unit = 50 ÷ 5
       = 10
 9 units = 10 × 9
        = 90
Mark had **$90** in the end.

10 Age difference → w years
Michelle's son is **(39 − w)** years old.

Chapter 6   Before and After – Change Unknown

1
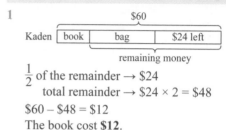

$\frac{1}{2}$ of the remainder → $24
    total remainder → $24 × 2 = $48
$60 − $48 = $12
The book cost **$12**.

2
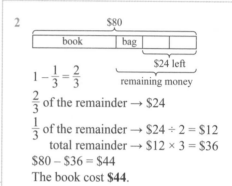

$1 - \frac{1}{3} = \frac{2}{3}$

$\frac{2}{3}$ of the remainder → $24

$\frac{1}{3}$ of the remainder → $24 ÷ 2 = $12
    total remainder → $12 × 3 = $36
$80 − $36 = $44
The book cost **$44**.

3 (a) Before

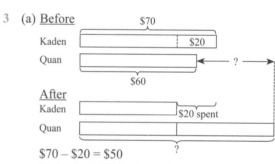

$70 − $20 = $50
Kaden had **$50** in the end.
(b) 2 × $50 = $100
Quan had $100 in the end.
$100 − $60 = $40
Quan received **$40** from mother.

4 (a) Before

Ryan

Kaden ⌐ $120

3 units = 120
 1 unit = 120 ÷ 3
      = 40
4 units = 40 × 4
      = 160
$160 + $40 = $200
$200 − $170 = $30
They had **$30** altogether in the end.

(b) After

Kaden ⎤
    ⎬ $30
Ryan ⎦

5 parts = $30
 1 part = $30 ÷ 5 = $6
2 parts = $6 × 2 = $12
Kaden had **$12** in the end.

5 (a) Before

Kaden

Quan

$15

Kaden at first → $15 × 3 = $45
total → $45 + $15 = $60
Kaden left → $45 − $10 = $35

After

Quan

Kaden

$35

5 units = $35
 1 unit = 35 ÷ 5
      = 7
4 units = 7 × 4
      = 28
Quan had **$28** in the end.

(b) $28 − $15 = $13
   Quan received **$13** from mother.

6 Before

Kaden ⎤
    ⎬ $279
Quan ⎦

9 units = 279
1 unit = 279 ÷ 9
     = 31
(Kaden) 2 units = 31 × 2
            = 62
(Quan) 7 units = 31 × 7
           = 217
Amount Kaden had in the end = $62 + $138
                    = $200

After

$200

Kaden

Quan

4 parts = $200
 1 part = $200 ÷ 4 = $50
7 parts = $50 × 7 = $350
$350 − $217 = $133
Quan received **$133** from his mother.

7 Total amount left after buying pencil case
   → $80 − $14
    = $66
   $100 − $66 = $34
   Keith received **$34** from father.

8 Before

$40\% = \frac{2}{5}$

male   female

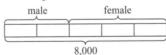

8,000

5 units = 8,000
 1 unit = 8,000 ÷ 5
      = 1,600
2 units = 1,600 × 2
      = 3,200
3 units = 1,600 × 3
      = 4,800
Women in the hall → 4,800 − 50 = 4,750

After

male

5 parts = 4,750
  1 part = 4,750 ÷ 5 = 950
8 parts = 950 × 8 = 7,600
8,000 − 7,600 = 400
400 people left the concert hall.

---

9 Before

$40\% = \dfrac{2}{5}$

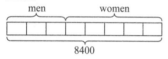

After

8 units = 8,400
  1 unit = 8,400 ÷ 8
      = 1,050
5 units = 1,050 × 5
      = 5,250
Number of women at first → 5,250 + 24 = 5,274

3 parts = 5,274
  1 part = 5,274 ÷ 3 = 1,758
5 parts = 1,758 × 5 = 8,790

8,790 − 8,400 = 390
390 people left the concert hall.

10

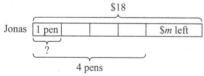

4 pens → $18 − $m = $(18 − m)$

1 pen → $\$\left(\dfrac{18-m}{4}\right)$

One pen cost $\$\left(\dfrac{18-m}{4}\right)$.

Chapter 7   Model Drawing – Transferring Part of the Model

1
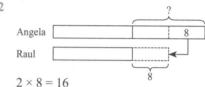

10 ÷ 2 = 5
Kaden must give **5** stamps to Ron.

2
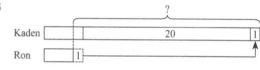

2 × 8 = 16
Angela had **16** more stickers than Raul at first.

3
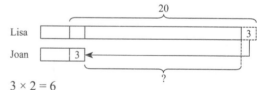

20 + 1 + 1 = 22
Kaden had **22** more stamps than Ron in the end.

4
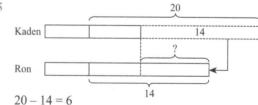

3 × 2 = 6
20 − 6 = 14
Lisa had **14** more apples than Joan in the end.

5
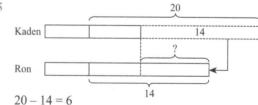

20 − 14 = 6
14 − 6 = 8
Kaden had **8** fewer stamps than Ron in the end.

6

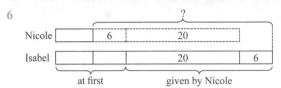

at first   given by Nicole

$26 + 6 = 32$

Nicole had **32** fewer cups than Isabel in the end.

7

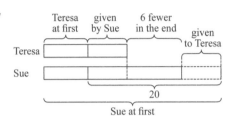

Sue at first

$20 - 6 = 14$
$14 \div 2 = 7$

Sue gave **7** cards to Teresa.

8 (a)

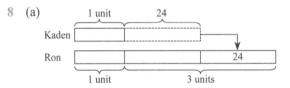

$24 + 24 = 48$
$3 \text{ units} = 48$
$1 \text{ unit} = 48 \div 3$
$\phantom{1 \text{ unit}} = 16$

Kaden had **16** stamps in the end.

(b) $4 \text{ units} = 16 \times 4$
$\phantom{4 \text{ units} } = 64$

Ron had **64** stamps in the end.

9

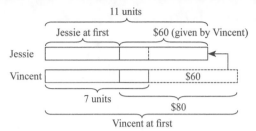

$\$80 - \$60 = \$20$
$\$60 - \$20 = \$40$
$4 \text{ units} = 40$
$1 \text{ unit} = 40 \div 4$
$\phantom{1 \text{ unit}} = 10$
$7 \text{ units} = 10 \times 7$
$\phantom{7 \text{ units}} = 70$
$\$70 + \$60 = \$130$

Vincent had **$130** at first.

10

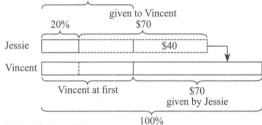

$\$70 - \$40 = \$30$
$\$30 + \$70 = \$100$
$100\% - 20\% = 80\%$
$80\% \rightarrow \$100$
Amount of money Jessie had in the end $\rightarrow 20\%$
$20\% \rightarrow \$100 \div 4$
$ = \$25$
$\$25 + \$70 = \$95$

Jessie had **$95** at first.

Chapter 8   Model Drawing – Comparing

1

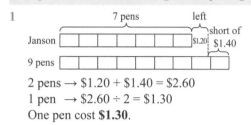

2 pens → $1.20 + $1.40 = $2.60
1 pen → $2.60 ÷ 2 = $1.30
One pen cost **$1.30**.

2

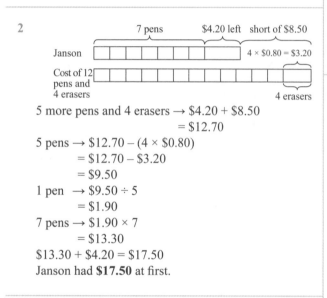

5 more pens and 4 erasers → $4.20 + $8.50
                          = $12.70
5 pens → $12.70 – (4 × $0.80)
       = $12.70 – $3.20
       = $9.50
1 pen → $9.50 ÷ 5
       = $1.90
7 pens → $1.90 × 7
       = $13.30
$13.30 + $4.20 = $17.50
Janson had **$17.50** at first.

3

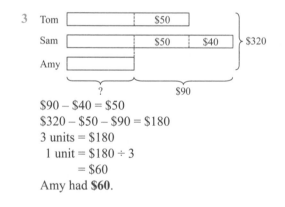

$90 – $40 = $50
$320 – $50 – $90 = $180
3 units = $180
 1 unit = $180 ÷ 3
        = $60
Amy had **$60**.

4 (a)

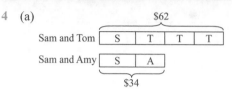

$62 – $34 = $28
Tom had **$28** more than Amy.
(b) 2 units = 28
    1 unit = 28 ÷ 2
           = 14
    3 units = 14 × 3
            = 42
Tom had **$42**.

5

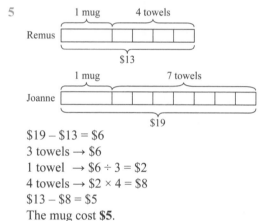

$19 – $13 = $6
3 towels → $6
1 towel → $6 ÷ 3 = $2
4 towels → $2 × 4 = $8
$13 – $8 = $5
The mug cost **$5**.

6

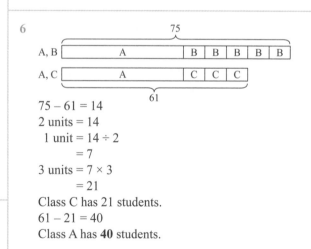

75 – 61 = 14
2 units = 14
 1 unit = 14 ÷ 2
        = 7
3 units = 7 × 3
        = 21
Class C has 21 students.
61 – 21 = 40
Class A has **40** students.

7   Difference in cost between 1 pencil and 1 eraser
    → $0.20
    Difference in cost between 10 pencils and 10 erasers
    → 10 × $0.20 = $2
    10 pencils cost $2 more than 10 erasers.

Cost of 10 pencils														

Cost of 10 pencils ☐☐☐☐☐☐☐☐☐☐
Cost of 10 erasers ☐☐☐☐☐☐☐☐☐☐ $2 more
Cost of 14 erasers ☐☐☐☐☐☐☐☐☐☐☐☐☐☐

    14 − 10 = 4
    Cost of 4 erasers → $2
    Cost of 1 eraser → $2 ÷ 2 = $0.50
    One eraser cost **$0.50**.

8   The difference between the number of items bought
    was that Logan bought 2 more pens than Christopher
    and Christopher bought 2 more markers then Logan.
    Logan spent $0.90 more and this means that 2 pens
    cost $0.90 more than 2 markers.
    Price difference between 1 pen and 1 marker
    → $0.90 ÷ 2 = $0.45
    The pen was **$0.45** more expensive than the marker.

9   14 − 6 = 8
    Remus bought 8 more apples than Jane.
    10 − 5 = 5
    Jane bought 5 more pears than Remus.
    As each of them spent the same amount of money, it
    means that the cost of 8 apples = the cost of 5 pears.
    Cost of 5 pears = Cost of 8 apples
    Cost of 10 pears = Cost of 16 apples
    6 + 16 = 22
    Jane could have bought **22** apples.

10 Vincent spent $9 less than Jessie = Jessie spent $9
    more than Vincent
    $17 − $9 = $8
    Jessie had $8 more than Vincent in the end.

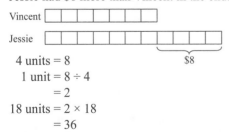

    4 units = 8
       1 unit = 8 ÷ 4
            = 2
    18 units = 2 × 18
            = 36
    Both of them had **$36** altogether in the end.

Chapter 9   Heuristic – Diagram Drawing

1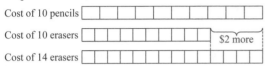

    Length → 4 units
    Width → 1 unit
    Perimeter → 2 Lengths + 2 Widths
              = 10 units
       10 units = 80 cm
          1 unit = 80 ÷ 10
               = 8
       4 units = 8 × 4
               = 32 cm
    The length of the rectangle is **32 cm**.

2
    Perimeter of 1 rectangle → 90 cm ÷ 2 = 45 cm
    Length → 3 units
    Width → 2 units
    Perimeter → 2 Lengths + 2 Widths
              = 10 units
       10 units = 45
          1 unit = 45 ÷ 10
               = 4.5
       2 units = 4.5 × 2
               = 9
    The width of the rectangle is **9 cm**.

3
    $1\frac{1}{4} = \frac{5}{4}$
    Width → 4 units
    Length → 5 units
    Perimeter → 2 Lengths + 2 Widths
              = 18 units
       18 units = 180
          1 unit = 180 ÷ 18
               = 10
    Width → 10 × 4 = 40
    Length → 10 × 5 = 50
    Area = Length × Width
         = 50 cm × 40 cm
         = 2,000 cm²
    The area of the rectangle is **2,000 cm²**.

4

Length → 4 units
Width → 3 units
Perimeter → 2 Lengths + 2 Widths
　　　　　= 14 units
　14 units = 70
　　1 unit = 70 ÷ 14
　　　　　= 5
Length → 5 × 4 = 20
Width → 5 × 3 = 15
Area = Length × Width
　　= 20 cm × 15 cm
　　= 300 cm²
The area of the rectangle is **300 cm²**.

5

Perimeter of 1 rectangle → 90 cm ÷ 3 = 30 cm
Length : Width
　100 : 50
　　2 : 1
Perimeter of 1 rectangle → 2 Lengths + 2 Widths
　　　　　　　　　　= 6 units
　　　　　6 units = 30
　　　　　1 unit = 30 ÷ 6
　　　　　　　　= 5
　　　　　2 units = 5 × 2
　　　　　　　　= 10
The length of 1 rectangle is **10 cm**.

6

Length : Width
　250 : 100
　　5 : 2
Perimeter → 2 Lengths + 2 Widths
　　　　　= 14
　14 units = 280
　　1 unit = 280 ÷ 14
　　　　　= 20
20 × 2 = 40
The width of the rectangle is **40 cm**.

7

Length : Width
　120 : 100
　　6 : 5
Perimeter → 2 Lengths + 2 Widths
　　　　　= 22
　22 units = 88
　　1 unit = 88 ÷ 22
　　　　　= 4
　6 units = 4 × 6
　　　　　= 24
The length of the rectangle is **24 cm**.

8　Length : Width
　　200 : 100
　　　2 : 1
Since the length is twice of its width, the rectangle is equal to 2 identical squares.
1u is 1 unit.

Area of 1 square → 98 ÷ 2 = 49
√49 = 7
The width of the rectangle is **7 cm**.

9

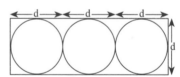

Length → 3 diameters (3d)
Width → 1 diameter (1d)
Perimeter → 2 Lengths + 2 Widths
　　　　　= (2 × 3d) + (2 × 1d)
　　　　　= 8d
　　　　8d = 80 cm
　　　　1d = 80 ÷ 8
　　　　　= 10 cm
Circumference of 1 circle = π × d
　　　　　　　　　　= 3.14 × 10 cm
　　　　　　　　　　= 31.4 cm
The circumference of 1 circle is **31.4 cm**.

10 Width → 2 diameters
Length → 4 diameters
1d = 1 diameter

Area of 1 square = 200 ÷ 8
= 25
1d = $\sqrt{25}$ = 5
Perimeter = (2 × 4d) + (2 × 2d)
= 12d
= 12 × 5
= 60
The perimeter of the rectangular cardboard is **60 cm**.

Chapter 10   Heuristic – Substituting

1    $1 - \frac{2}{5} = \frac{5}{5} - \frac{2}{5} = \frac{3}{5}$ (Fraction of money left)

$\frac{2}{5}$ of Irene's money → 10 pens

$\frac{3}{5}$ of Irene's money → 15 pens

24 – 15 = 9
9 pens → $18
  1 pen → $18 ÷ 9 = $2
15 pens $\left(\frac{3}{5}\text{ of Irene's money}\right)$ → $2 × 15 = $30
Irene had **$30** left after buying the 10 pens.

2   Cost of 1 orange → 1 unit
Cost of 1 pear → 1 unit + $0.10
Cost of 15 pears → (1 unit + $0.10) × 15
= 15 units + (15 × $0.10)
= 15 units + $1.50
Cost of 18 oranges → 18 units
15 units + $1.50 = 18 units (Cost of 15 pears = Cost
of 18 oranges)
18 units – 15 units = 3 units
3 units (3 oranges) → $1.50
1 orange → $0.50
1 pear → $0.50 + $0.10 = $0.60
15 pears → $0.60 × 15 = $9
Willy spent **$9** on the 15 pears.

3   1L = 1 large box
1S = 1 small box
1L = 1S + 20
2L = 2S + 40
6S = 2 × (2S + 40)
6S = 4S + 80
2S = 80
1S = 40
1L = 40 + 20 = 60
One large box has **60** nails.

4   $80 - 30 = 50$
    Andy took 50 days took to finish reading.
    $50 \times 3 = 150$
    Andy read 150 pages more than Marcus in 50 days.
    $150 \div 30 = 5$
    Marcus read 5 pages each day.
    $80 \times 5 = 400$
    The storybook had **400** pages.

5   $\div 6 \Big($ Cost of 24 cards = Cost of 30 stickers $\Big) \div 6$
    $\times 2 \Big($ Cost of 4 cards = Cost of 5 stickers $\Big) \times 2$
    $\quad \Big($ Cost of 8 cards = Cost of 10 stickers
    Amy's money = John's money
    Amy's money = Cost of 30 stickers
    $30 - 10 = 20$
    Amy bought buy **20** stickers.

6   Ben at first → 1 unit
    Jann at first → 5 units
    Ben in the end → 1 unit + 4
    Jann in the end → 5 units − 4
    Jann in the end (Since Jann has three times as many as Ben)
    → $3 \times (1 \text{ unit} + 4) = 3 \text{ units} + 12$
    $3 \text{ units} + 12 = 5 \text{ units} - 4$
    $2 \text{ units} = 12 + 4 = 16$
    $1 \text{ unit} = 16 \div 2 = 8$
    $5 \text{ units} = 8 \times 5 = 40$
    $40 - 4 = 36$
    Jann had **36** books in the end.

7

Nicole	Hannah
1 unit	3 units
+4	+3
1 p	2 p

$\times 2 \Big($ 1 unit + 4 = 1 part $\Big) \times 2$
$\quad \Big($ 2 units + 8 = 2 parts
$3 \text{ units} + 3 = 2 \text{ parts} = 2 \text{ units} + 8$
$3 \text{ units} + 3 = 2 \text{ units} + 8$
$1 \text{ unit} = 5$
$1 \text{ part} = 5 + 4 = 9$
$2 \text{ parts} = 2 \times 9 = 18$
Hannah had **18** apples in the end.

8   Magnets Nicole had at first → 2 units
    Magnets Nicole had in the end → 2 units + 4
    Magnets Hannah had at first → 3 units
    Magnets Hannah had in the end → 3 units + 13
    Hannah had twice as many as Nicole in the end
    → $2 \times (2 \text{ units} + 4)$
    $= 4 \text{ units} + 8$
    $3 \text{ units} + 13 = 4 \text{ units} + 8$
    $\quad 1 \text{ unit} = 5$
    $\quad 3 \text{ units} = 5 \times 3$
    $\quad\quad\quad = 15$
    $15 + 13 = 28$
    Hannah had **28** magnets in the end.

9   1 cupcake = 2 cookies
    7 cupcakes = 14 cookies
    14 cookies + 4 cookies = 18 cookies
    30% → 18 cookies
    10% → 6 cookies
    70% → 42 cookies
    $\frac{6}{7} \times 42 \text{ cookies} = 36 \text{ cookies}$
    $36 - 10 = 26$
    $26 \div 2 = 13$
    26 cookies = 13 cupcakes
    She bought **13** cupcakes on Tuesday.

10 $100\% + 50\% = 150\%$
    $150 : 100$
    $\quad 3 : 2$
    1 mango → 3 units
    1 apple → 2 units
    $7 \times 2 \text{ units} = 14 \text{ units}$ (7 apples)
    $2 \times 3 \text{ units} = 6 \text{ units}$ (2 mangoes)
    14 units + 6 units = 20 units (7 apples and 2 mangoes)
    25% → 20 units
    75% → 60 units
    100% of remaining → 60 units
    80% of remaining → $\frac{60}{100} \times 80$
    $\quad\quad\quad\quad\quad = 48 \text{ units}$
    $48 \text{ units} \div 3 \text{ units} = 16$
    Sue could buy **16** more mangoes with 80% of her remaining money.

Review 1 – Chapters 1 to 10

1 Jeremy and Randy are both older by 4 years now.
This means the sum of their age had increased by 4 ×
2 = 8 years now.
Total age now → 30 + 8 = 38
Their total age is **38** years.

2 <u>Before</u>

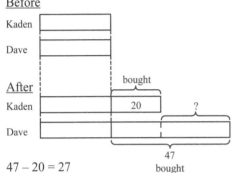

47 − 20 = 27
Dave had **27** more game cards than Kaden in the end.

3 <u>Before</u>

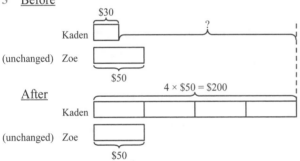

To have 4 times as much money as Zoe,
Kaden must have → $50 × 4 = $200
Kaden had $30, so he would need another
→ $200 − $30 = $170
Kaden must have **$170** more.

4 Total number of stamps in the end → 207 + 3 − 3
= 207
Total number of stamps in the end = Total number of
stamps at first
(The number of stamps Christopher bought was the
same as the number of stamps Andy lost.)
They had **207** stamps in the end.

5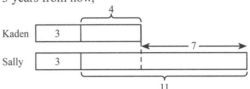

11 − 4 = 7
They are **7** years apart.
3 years from now,

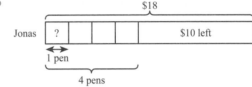

They are **7** years apart.

6

$18 − $10 = $8
4 pens → $8
1 pen → $8 ÷ 4 = $2
One pen cost **$2**.

7

(Since Kaden gave 3 stamps to Ron, he would have
fewer stamps than Ron as shown in the model
drawing.)
2 × 3 = 6
Ron would have **6** more stamps than Kaden.

8

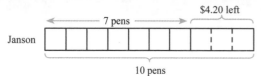

$10 - 7 = 3$
3 pens → \$4.20
1 pen → \$4.20 ÷ 3 = \$1.40
10 pens → \$1.40 × 10 = \$14
He had **\$14**.

9

Length → 3 units
Width → 1 unit
Perimeter → 2 Lengths + 2 Widths
    = 3 units + 3 units + 1 unit + 1 unit
    = 8 units
8 units = 72
1 unit = 72 ÷ 8
    = 9
3 units = 9 × 3
    = 27
The length of the rectangle is **27 cm**.

10 1 jug = 4 cups
2 jugs = 8 cups

1 cup

1 jug

1 cup 1 cup 1 cup 1 cup

Substituting the 2 jugs for 8 cups,
8 cups + 10 cups = 18 cups
1 cup → 3600 ml ÷ 18 = 200 ml
4 cups → 200 ml × 4 = 800 ml
1 jug → 800 ml = 0.8 L
A jug can hold **0.8** L.

Chapter 11 Heuristic – Working Backwards

1 Before

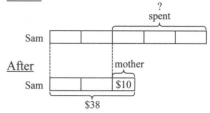

$38 - $10 = $28
2 units = 28
 1 unit = 28 ÷ 2
    = 14
3 units = 14 × 3
    = 42
Sam spent **\$42**.

2 Before

gave to James

Kelvin

After

Kelvin

\$140

5 units = 140
 1 unit = 140 ÷ 5
    = 28
2 units = 28 × 2
    = 56
James received \$56 from Kelvin.
\$100 − \$56 = \$44
James had **\$44** at first.

3 After
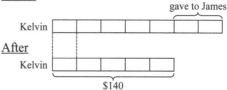
$$1 - \frac{1}{5} = \frac{5}{5} - \frac{1}{5}$$
$$= \frac{4}{5}$$

$\frac{4}{5}$ of Kaden's original money

Kaden

Dan

\$240

Dan's money at first   given by Kaden

8 units = 240
 1 unit = 240 ÷ 8
    = 30
3 units = 30 × 3
    = 90
Dan had **\$90** at first.

4 <u>After</u>

5 units = 200
 1 unit = 200 ÷ 5
     = 40
Kaden had $40 in the end.
4 units = 40 × 4
     = 160
Dan had $160 in the end.

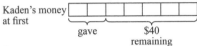

$\frac{5}{7}$ of Kaden's money at first → $40

$\frac{1}{7}$ of Kaden's money at first → $40 ÷ 5 = $8

Kaden gave to Dan $\frac{2}{7}$ of his money.

$\frac{2}{7}$ of Kaden's money at first → $8 × 2 = $16

$160 – $16 = $144
Dan had **$144** at first.

5

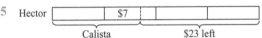

3 units = $7 + $23
     = $30
 1 unit = $30 ÷ 3
     = $10
4 units = $10 × 4
     = $40
Hector had **$40** at first.

6

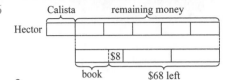

$\frac{2}{3}$ of remaining amount of money → $68 – $8
               = $60

$\frac{1}{3}$ of remaining amount of money → $60 ÷ 2
               = $30

Total remaining amount of money → $30 × 3
               = $90

5 units = 90
 1 unit = 90 ÷ 5
     = 18
Hector's original money, 6 units = $18 × 6
               = $108

Hector had **$108** at first.

7

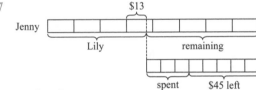

$1 - \frac{3}{8} = \frac{5}{8}$

$\frac{5}{8}$ of remaining money → $45

$\frac{1}{8}$ of remaining money → $45 ÷ 5 = $9

$\frac{8}{8}$ of remaining money → $9 × 8 = $72

$\frac{5}{8}$ of original sum of money → $72 + $13 = $85

$\frac{1}{8}$ of original sum of money → $85 ÷ 5 = $17

Total amount → $17 × 8 = $136
Jenny had **$136** at first.

8

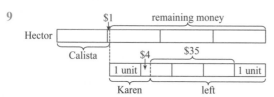

$17 + $1 = $18
3 units = 18
  1 unit = 18 ÷ 3
        = 6
7 units = 6 × 7
        = 42
$42 + $9 = $51
3 parts = $51
1 part = $51 ÷ 3 = $17
5 parts = $17 × 5 = $85
Emma had **$85** at first.

9

Hector | $1 | remaining money
Calista | $4 | $35
1 unit | | 1 unit
Karen | left

Karen's money → 1 unit + $4
Hector left → Karen's money + $31 more
            = (1 unit + $4) + $31
            = 1 unit + $35
3 units = $35 + $4
        = $39
  1 unit = $39 ÷ 3
        = $13
5 units = $13 × 5
        = $65
$65 + $1 = $66
$\frac{3}{4}$ of Hector's money at first → $66
$\frac{1}{4}$ of Hector's money at first → $66 ÷ 3
                                      = $22
$22 + $1 = $23
Hector gave Calista **$23**.

10

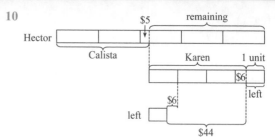

2 units = $44 − $6 − $6 = $32
1 unit = $32 ÷ 2 = $16
4 units = $16 × 4 = $64
Remaining amount of money → $64
$64 + $5 = $69
$\frac{3}{5}$ of Hector's money → $69
$\frac{1}{5}$ of Hector's money → $69 ÷ 3 = $23
$\frac{2}{5}$ of Hector's money → $23 × 2 = $46
$46 + $5 = $51
Hector gave Calista **$51**.

Chapter 12   Heuristic – Logical Reasoning

1   To make the largest possible sum, choose the largest pair of two digits where the difference is 4.
Choosing the largest possible digit → 9
The smaller digit → 9 – 4 = 5
Largest possible sum → 5 + 9 = **14**

2   Sum of 4 digits → 6 × 4 = 24
Sum of the other 2 digits → 24 – 8 – 3 = 13
Largest digit possible → 9
Smaller digit → 13 – 9 = 4
Largest difference → 9 – 4 = **5**

3   Sum of 3 numbers → 61 × 3 = 183
Sum of 2 numbers → 183 – 33 = 150
Largest number possible → 99
Smaller number → 150 – 99 = 51
Largest difference → 99 – 51 = **48**

4   Sum of 3 numbers → 45 × 3 = 135
Sum of other 2 numbers → 135 – 70 = 65
Smallest number possible → 10
Larger number → 65 – 10 = 55
Largest difference → 55 – 10 = **45**

5   Sum of 3 numbers → 39 × 3 = 117
Sum of other 2 numbers → 117 – 65 = 52
Smallest odd number possible → 11
Larger number → 52 – 11 = 41
Largest difference → 41 – 11 = **30**

6   Sum of three numbers → 80 × 3 = 240
Sum of other two numbers → 240 – 76 = 164
Largest number possible → 98
Smaller number → 164 – 98 = 66
Largest difference → 98 – 66 = **32**

7   Sum of four numbers → 500 × 4 = 2,000
Sum of other 2 numbers → 2000 – 150 – 230 = 1,620
Largest number possible → 999
Smaller number → 1,620 – 999 = 621
Largest difference → 999 – 621 = **378**

8   Sum of four numbers → 201 × 4 = 804
Sum of other two numbers → 804 – 301 – 203 = 300
Smallest number possible → 101
Larger number → 300 – 101 = 199
Largest difference → 199 – 101 = **98**

9   Smallest A → 8 × 2 = 16
Largest A → 8 × 12 = 96
Smallest B → 20 × 1 = 20
Largest B → 20 × 4 = 80
Difference between Largest A and Smallest B
= 96 – 20
= 76
Difference between Largest B and Smallest A
= 80 – 16
= 64
Largest possible difference = **76**.

10 Smallest X → 2 × 5 + 2 = 12
Largest X → 19 × 5 + 2 = 97
Smallest Y → 1 × 20 + 3 = 23
Largest Y → 4 × 20 + 3 = 83
Difference between Largest X and Smallest Y
→ 97 – 23
= 74
Difference between Largest Y and Smallest X
→ 83 – 12
= 71
Largest possible difference = **74**

Chapter 13   Heuristic – Geometrical Visualisation

1   Triangle GEF = Triangle GEC

$\angle GCE = \angle GFE$

$\angle GCE = 90º$

$\angle GFE = 90º$

$\angle FEG = 180º - 90º - 20º = 70º$

$\angle FEG = \angle GEC$ (Folded)

$\angle y = 180º - 70º - 70º = \mathbf{40º}$

2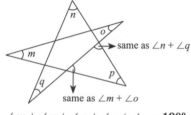

same as $\angle n + \angle q$

same as $\angle m + \angle o$

$\angle m + \angle n + \angle o + \angle p + \angle q = \mathbf{180º}$

3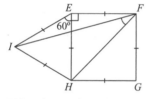

Triangle EFI is an isosceles triangle

$\angle IEF = 60º + 90º$

$= 150º$

$\angle EFI = (180º - 150º) \div 2$

$= 15º$

$\angle EFH = 45º$ ($EFGH$ is a square)

$\angle IFH = 45º - 15º$

$= \mathbf{30º}$

4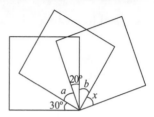

$\angle a = 90º - 30º - 20º$

$= 40º$

$\angle b = 90º - 40º - 20º$

$= 30º$

$\angle x = 90º - 20º - 30º$

$= \mathbf{40º}$

5

$\angle a = (180º - 20º) \div 2$

$= 80º$

$\angle b = 180º - 90º - 80º$

$= 10º$

$\angle c = 90º - 10º - 10º$

$= 70º$

$\angle x = 180º - 70º - 90º$

$= \mathbf{20º}$

6   Triangle XYZ is an equilateral triangle as XY, YZ and ZX are all the diagonals of the square faces on the cube, therefore they are of the same length.

$\angle XYZ = 180º \div 3$

$= \mathbf{60º}$

7    $\angle GFH = \angle GFI$ (Folded)

$\angle GFI = (60º - 18º) \div 2 = 21º$

$\angle y = 180º - 21º - 60º$

$= \mathbf{99º}$

8    $\angle a + \angle b = 180º - 20º$

$= 160º$

$\angle c + \angle d = 180º - 20º$

$= 160º$

$\angle e + \angle f = 180º - 20º$

$= 160º$

$\angle a + \angle b + \angle c + \angle d + \angle e + \angle f = 160º \times 3$

$= \mathbf{480º}$

9

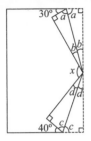

$\square a = (180° - 30°) \div 2$
$\quad = 75°$
$\square b = 180° - 90° - 75°$
$\quad = 15°$
$\square c = (180° - 40°) \div 2$
$\quad = 70°$
$\square d = 180° - 90° - 70°$
$\quad = 20°$
$\square x = 180° - 15° - 15° - 20° - 20°$
$\quad = \mathbf{110°}$

10

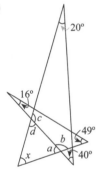

$\square b = 180° - 16° - 49°$
$\quad = 115°$
$\square a = 180° - 115°$
$\quad = 65°$
$\square c = 180° - 20° - 40°$
$\quad = 120°$
$\square d = 180° - 120°$
$\quad = 60°$
$\square x = 180° - 65° - 60°$
$\quad = \mathbf{55°}$

Chapter 14   Concept – Pairing

1   $\$21 \div \$3 = 7$ (Pairs of muffin and tart)
$2 \times 7 = 14$
Alice bought **14** muffins and tarts.

2   $\$0.20 + \$1 = \$1.20$
The total value of 1 twenty-cent coin and 1 one-dollar coin is **$1.20**.
$\$36 \div \$1.20 = 30$ (pairs)
$2 \times 30 = 60$
Adam has **60** coins.

3   Cost of 2 more tarts $\rightarrow 2 \times \$1 = \$2$
$\$14.50 - \$2 = \$12.50$ (Cost of same number of muffins and tarts)
$\$1.50 + \$1 = \$2.50$ (Cost of 1 pair of muffin and tart)
$\$12.50 \div \$2.50 = 5$ (pairs)
$2 \times 5 = 10$
$10 + 2 = 12$
Alice bought **12** muffins and tarts.

4   $\$6.20 - \$0.20 = \$6$ (Cost of same number of each type of coins)
$\$0.20 + \$1 = \$1.20$ (Value of 1 pair)
$\$6 \div \$1.20 = 5$ (pairs)
$5 \times 1 = 5$
$5 + 1 = 6$
Ethan has **6** twenty-cent coins.

5   $4 \times \$1 = \$4$
$\$7 + \$4 = \$11$ (Cost of same number of each type of coins by adding 4 more one-dollar coins)
$\$1 + \$0.10 = \$1.10$ (Value of 1 pair)
$\$11 \div \$1.10 = 10$ (pairs)
$10 \times 2 = 20$ (coins in 10 pairs)
$20 - 4 = 16$ (Take away the 4 coins added)
Lucas has **16** coins in all.

6   $\$1 - \$0.20 = \$0.80$
40 coins $\div$ 2 coins of each type = 20 pairs
20 pairs $\times \$0.80 = \$16$
The difference is **$16**.

7 $1 − $0.20 = $0.80 (Difference between 1 pair of $1 coin and 20¢ coin)
$7.20 ÷ $0.80 = 9 (pairs)
9 pairs × 2 coins of each type = 18 coins in all
Adam has **18** coins in all.

8 When the value of 1 twenty-cent coin is removed from all the coins, the difference in value between all the one-dollar coins and twenty-cent coins is
→ $5.40 + $0.20
= $5.60
$1 − $0.20 = $0.80 (Difference between each pair)
$5.60 ÷ $0.80 = 7 (pairs)
7 × 2 = 14 (Coins in 7 pairs)
14 + 1 = 15 (Replacing the twenty-cent coin)
Jacob has **15** coins altogether.

9 3 × $10 = $30 (Value of the 3 more $10 bills)
Difference → $94 − $30
= $64 (Take away the 3 more $10 bills)
$10 − $2 = $8 (Difference between 1 pair of $10 and $2 bills)
$64 ÷ $8 = 8 pairs
Mason has **8** $2 bills.

10 3 × $1 = $3
Difference in value after adding 3 one-dollar coins
→ $7.80 + $3
= $10.80
$1 − $0.10 = $0.90 (Difference in value for 1 pair of $1 coin and 10¢ coin)
$10.80 ÷ $0.90 = 12 (Pairs)
2 × 12 = 24 (Coins in 12 pairs)
24 − 3 = 21 (Remove 3 one-dollar coins)
Adam has **21** coins in all.

Chapter 15 Concept – Grouping

1 1 group → 4 × $2 bill + 1 × $5 bill
= Total value of ($8 + $5)
= $13
$91 ÷ $13 = 7 (Number of groups)
7 × 4 = 28
Ramesh had a total of **28** $2 bills.

2 1 group → 1 × $2 bill + 3 × $5 bill
= Total value of ($2 + $15)
= $17
$136 ÷ $17 = 8 (Number of groups)
8 × 3 = 24
Ramesh has a total of **24** $5 bills.

3 1 group → 2 oranges + 3 apples
Cost of 1 group → 2 × ($0.50 + $0.10) + 3 × $0.50
= $2.70
$10.80 ÷ $2.70 = 4 (Number of groups)
3 × 4 = 12
Sue bought **12** apples.

4 1 group → 2 oranges + 3 apples
Difference in cost in 1 group
→ 3 × $0.50 − 2 × ($0.50 + $0.10)
= $1.50 − $1.20
= $0.30
$1.80 ÷ $0.30 = 6 (Number of groups)
(2 + 3) × 6 = 5 × 6
= 30
Sue bought **30** fruit altogether.

5 1 group → 2 wins + 1 draw
Points for a group of 2 wins and 1 draw
→ 2 × 3 + 1 × 1
= 7
No points were scored for any losses, so all the 70 points must be due to the wins and draws, which were in groups of 2 wins and 1 draw.
70 ÷ 7 = 10 (Number of groups)
3 × 10 = 30 (Total wins and draws)
38 − 30 = 8
The team lost **8** games.

6   Since there are three times as many $5 bills as $10 bills,
1 group → 3 × $5 bill and 1 × $10 bill
Since there are four times as many $2 bills as $5 bills and there are three times as many $5 bills as $10 bills,
1 group → (4 × 3) × $2 bill, 3 × $5 bill and
              1 × $10 bill
           = 12 × $2 bill, 3 × $5 bill and
              1 × $10 bill
Value of 1 group of 12 $2 bills and 1 $10 bills
→ 2 × $12 + $10
 = $24 + $10
 = $34
$306 ÷ $34 = 9 (Number of groups)
3 × 9 = 27
There are **27** $5 bills in Ken's wallet.

7   In order for the 10-cent coins to be equal in value with the one-dollar coin,
1 group → 10 × 10-cent coins + 1 one-dollar coin
Number of coins in 1 group → 10 + 1
                                   = 11
88 ÷ 11 = 8 (Number of groups)
10 × 8 = 80
There are **80** 10-cent coins altogether.

8   Cost of 1 pencil → 2 units
Cost of 1 eraser → 3 units
In order for the total cost of all the pencils to be 4 times as much as the total cost of all the erasers,
3 units × 4 = 12 units (4 times the cost of 1 eraser)
12 units ÷ 2 units = 6
Every 1 eraser must be matched with 6 pencils
(1 group).
1 group → 6 + 1 = 7
35 ÷ 7 = 5 (Number of groups)
6 × 5 = 30
Tom bought **30** pencils altogether.

9   Adjust the number of $5 bills to be the same as $2 bills by removing 3 $2 bills and add 3 $5 bills.
$159 − 3 × $2 + 3 × $5 = $168

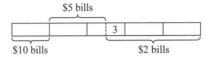

1 group → 1 × $10 bill, 2 × $5 bill and
              2 × $2 bill
Value of 1 group → $10 + $10 + $4 = $24
$168 ÷ $24 = 7 (Number of groups)
7 × 2 = 14
14 + 3 = 17
There were **17** $2 bills altogether.

10 $\frac{75}{100} = \frac{3}{4}$ (For every group of 4 students, 3 answered 48 questions correctly.)
44 × 4 = 176 (Total number of questions answered correctly for a group of 4 students)
176 − 3 × 48 = 32
The average number of questions that were answered incorrectly by the bottom 25% of the participants was **32**.

Chapter 16 Concept – Division with Remainder

1 $32 \div 3 = 10\ R\ 2$
$10 + 1 = 11$
$11 \times \$4 = \$44$
Owen will have to pay **$44**.

2 $\$25 \div \$4 = 6\ R\ 1$
$3 \times 6 = 18$
I can buy **18** muffins.

3 $\$19 \div \$3 = 6\ R\ \$1$
$6 \times 2 = 12$
I can buy **12** cookies.

4 $\$22 \div \$5 = 4\ R\ \$2$
$3 \times 4 = 12$
Owen can buy **12** muffins and he will have **$2** left.

5 $22 \div (3 + 1) = 5\ R\ 2$
5 groups of 3 muffins bought and 1 muffin given free.
5 groups × 1 free muffin = 5 free muffins
$22 - 5 = 17$
17 muffins → $17 \times \$1.50 = \$25.50$
She needs **$25.50**.

6 $2 \times \$1.30 = \$2.60$
$\$2.60 + \$1 = \$3.60$
$\$17 \div \$3.60 = 4\ R\ \$2.60$
$\$2.60 \div \$1.30 = 2$
$4 \times 3 = 12$
$12 + 2 = 14$
Owen can buy a maximum of **14** cupcakes.

7 $5 \times \$1.60 = \$8$
$2 \times \$0.30 = \$0.60$
$\$8 - \$0.60 = \$7.40$ (1 group of 3 ice cream cones at original price and 2 ice cream cones at discounted price)
$\$24 \div \$7.40 = 3\ R\ \$1.80$
$\$1.80 \div \$1.60 = 1\ R\ \$0.20$
$3 \times 5 = 15$
$15 + 1 = 16$
Owen can buy **16** ice cream cones and he will have **$0.20** left.

8 1 week of earnings → $5 \times \$100 + 2 \times \$120$
$= \$740$
$\$4,740 \div \$740 = 6\ R\ \$300$
$6 \times 7 = 42$
$\$300 \div \$100 = 3$
$42 + 3 = 45$
The substitute teacher has to work for **45** days.

9 $\$23 \div \$0.50 = 46$ (days needed to save $23)
$46 \div 7 = 6\ R\ 4$ (6 weeks and 4 days)
6 groups of Wed, Thu, Fri, Sat, Sun, Mon, and Tue.
Remaining 4 days → Wed, Thu, Fri and Sat.
Connie would have saved a total of $23 in her piggy bank on **Saturday**.

10 $(5 \times \$1) + (2 \times \$2) = \$9$
$\$32 \div \$9 = 3\ R\ \$5$
3 groups of Fri, Sat, Sun, Mon, Tue, Wed, and Thu.
Remaining $5 → Fri ($1), Sat ($2), and Sun ($2).
Connie would have saved a total of $32 in her piggy bank on **Sunday**.

Chapter 17   Concept – Gaps and Intervals

1. $9 - 1 = 8$ (Total number of gaps)
$8 \times 20 \text{ m} = 160 \text{ m}$
The distance from the first street lamp to the last street lamp was **160 m.**

2. Number of gaps will always be 1 fewer than number of pupils.
$12 - 1 = 11$ (Number of gaps from the first to the last pupil)
$66 \div 11 = 6$ (Length of each gap)
The distance between every two pupils was **6 m**.

3. Number of gaps between 2nd and 6th pupil
$\rightarrow 6 - 2 = 4$
$20 \text{ m} \div 4 = 5 \text{ m}$ (Length of each gap)
$10 - 1 = 9$ (Total number of gaps)
$9 \times 5 \text{ m} = 45 \text{ m}$
The distance between the first pupil and the last pupil was **45 m**.

4. Number of gaps between 3rd and 8th pupil
$\rightarrow 8 - 3 = 5$
$10 \text{ m} \div 5 = 2 \text{ m}$ (Length of each gap)
$30 \text{ m} \div 2 \text{ m} = 15$ (Total number of gaps)
$15 + 1 = 16$
There were **16** pupils standing in the row altogether.

5. $13 - 9 = 4$ (Number of gaps from 9th to 13th potted plants)
$24 \text{ m} \div 4 = 6 \text{ m}$
$78 \text{ m} \div 6 \text{ m} = 13$ (Total number of gaps)
$13 + 1 = 14$
There were **14** potted plants placed altogether.

6. $9 - 1 = 8$ (Number of gaps along one side of the square garden)
$8 \times 5 \text{ m} = 40 \text{ m}$ (Length of one side of square garden)
$4 \times 40 \text{ m} = 160 \text{ m}$
The perimeter of the square garden was **160 m**.

7. $21 - 1 = 20$ (Total number of gaps on Road A)
$20 \times 10 \text{ m} = 200 \text{ m}$ (Length of both roads)
$21 - 4 = 17$ (Street lamps on Road B)
$17 - 1 = 16$ (Number of gaps on Road B)
$200 \text{ m} \div 16 = 12.5$ (Distance between every 2 street lamps on Road B)
The distance between every 2 street lamps on Road B was **12.5 m**.

8. $11 - 7 = 4$ (Number of gaps between 7th street lamp and 11th street lamp)
$80 \text{ m} \div 4 = 20 \text{ m}$ (Length of gap on Road A)
$25 - 1 = 24$ (Total number of gaps on Road A)
$24 \times 20 \text{ m} = 480 \text{ m}$ (Length of road)
$25 + 6 = 31$ (Total number of street lamps on Road B)
$31 - 1 = 30$ (Total number of gaps on Road B)
$480 \text{ m} \div 30 = 16 \text{ m}$ (Length of gap between every 2 street lamps on Road B)
The distance between every 2 street lamps on Road B was **16 m**.

9. $36 \times 20 \text{ cm} = 720 \text{ cm}$ (Total length of the 36 flags)
$36 - 1 = 35$ (Total number of gaps at first)
$35 \times 66 \text{ cm} = 2{,}310 \text{ cm}$ (Total length of the gaps)
$2{,}310 \text{ cm} + 720 \text{ cm} = 3{,}030 \text{ cm}$
   (Total length of all the flags and gaps at first)
$8 + 36 = 44$ (Total number of flags in the end)
$44 \times 20 \text{ cm} = 880 \text{ cm}$ (Total length of the flags in the end)
$3{,}030 \text{ cm} - 880 \text{ cm} = 2{,}150 \text{ cm}$ (Total length of all the gaps in the end)
$2{,}150 \text{ cm} \div (44 - 1) = 50 \text{ cm}$ (Length of 1 gap)
The spacing between every 2 flags on the second string was **50 cm**.

10. $16 - 10 = 6$ (Number of gaps from 10th to 16th levels)
$6 \times 2.5 \text{ m} = 15 \text{ m}$ (Total distance travelled by lift in 3 s)
$15 \text{ m} \div 3 \text{ s} = 5 \text{ m/s}$
The speed of the lift is **5 m/s**.

Chapter 18   Concept – Fractions of Different Sets

1

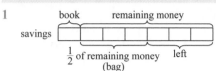

Savings → 7 units
Remaining amount of money → 7 – 1 = 6
Bag ($\frac{1}{2}$ of remaining amount of money) → 6 ÷ 2 = 3
Left → 7 – 1 – 3 = 3
$\frac{3}{7}$ of his savings was left.

2

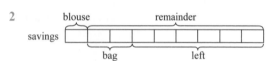

Remainder → 9 – 1 = 8
Bag ($\frac{1}{4}$ of remainder) → 8 ÷ 4 = 2
Left → 9 – 1 – 2 = 6
$\frac{6^{÷3}}{9_{÷3}} = \frac{2}{3}$
$\frac{2}{3}$ of her savings was left.

3

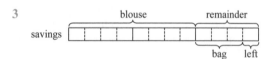

$\frac{1}{12}$ of her savings was left.

4

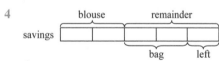

$\frac{1}{5}$ of her savings was left.

5

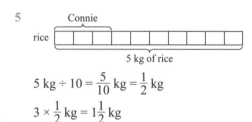

$5 \text{ kg} ÷ 10 = \frac{5}{10} \text{ kg} = \frac{1}{2} \text{ kg}$

$3 × \frac{1}{2} \text{ kg} = 1\frac{1}{2} \text{ kg}$

Jason gave Connie **$1\frac{1}{2}$ kg** of rice.

6

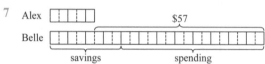

$1 - \frac{1}{3} = \frac{2}{3}$

$\frac{2}{3}$ of Alex's money = $\frac{4}{5}$ of Belle's money
$\frac{4}{6}$ of Alex's money = $\frac{4}{5}$ of Belle's money

Total → 6 units + 5 units = 11 units
11 units = $88
 1 unit = $88 ÷ 11 = $8
 2 units = $8 × 2 = $16
Alex saved **$16**.

7

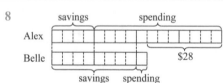

Alex → 5 units
Belle → 24 units
Difference → 24 units – 5 units = 19 units
19 units = $57
 1 unit = $57 ÷ 19 = $3
(Belle's spending) 16 units = $3 × 16 = $48
Belle spent **$48**.

8

Alex → 16 units
Belle → 9 units
Difference → 16 units – 9 units = 7 units
7 units = $28
1 unit = $28 ÷ 7 = $4
9 units = $4 × 9 = $36
Belle had **$36** at first.

9

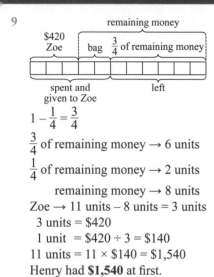

$1 - \frac{1}{4} = \frac{3}{4}$

$\frac{3}{4}$ of remaining money → 6 units

$\frac{1}{4}$ of remaining money → 2 units

     remaining money → 8 units

Zoe → 11 units − 8 units = 3 units

 3 units = $420

 1 unit = $420 ÷ 3 = $140

11 units = 11 × $140 = $1,540

Henry had **$1,540** at first.

10   Blue → $\frac{3}{7} = \frac{15}{35}$

Given away → $\frac{2}{5} = \frac{14}{35}$

Left → $1 - \frac{14}{35} = \frac{21}{35}$

Green buttons left → $\frac{2}{3} \times \frac{21}{35} = \frac{14}{35}$

Blue buttons left → $\frac{21}{35} - \frac{14}{35} = \frac{7}{35}$

Blue buttons given away → $\frac{15}{35} - \frac{7}{35} = \frac{8}{35}$

$\frac{8}{35}$ of buttons → 80

$\frac{1}{35}$ of buttons → 10

Buttons → 10 × 35 = 350

Ryan had **350** buttons altogether at first.

Chapter 19   Concept – Finding Relationships

1   Difference in units between Kaden and John in the end → 5 − 2 = 3

3 units = 21

 1 unit = 21 ÷ 3

    = 7

(Kaden left) → 2 units = 7 × 2

          = 14

(John left) → 5 units = 7 × 5

          = 35

John gave away → 35 + 4 = 39

John gave away : Kaden gave away = 3 : 5

                    = 39 : 65

14 + 65 = 79

Kaden had **79** marbles at first.

2   Marbles Kaden gave away → 1 unit

Marbles John gave away → 2 units

Marbles John had left → 2 units (Same as number of marbles John gave away as stated in question)

Marbles Kaden had left → 2 × 2 units = 4 units

Total marbles → $\underbrace{1 \text{ unit} + 2 \text{ units}}_{\text{given away}} + \underbrace{2 \text{ units} + 4 \text{ units}}_{\text{left}}$

          = 9 units

9 units = 108

 1 unit = 108 ÷ 9

    = 12

Total marbles John had → 2 units + 2 units

              = 4 units

4 units = 12 × 4

    = 48

John had **48** marbles at first.

3   Kaden left → 1 unit

Adam left → 2 units

John left → 2 × 2 units = 4 units

Total left → 1 unit + 2 units + 4 units = 7 units

7 units = 56

 1 unit = 8

Kaden gave away → 8 − 2 = 6

2 parts = 6

 1 part = 6 ÷ 2

    = 3

9 parts = 3 × 9

    = 27

John gave away **27** marbles.

          Singapore Math Challenge Word Problems

4   Number of marbles Isaac had left → 1 unit
Number of marbles Leo had left → 1 unit + 2
Number of marbles Isaac had given away
→ 1 unit + 5
Number of marbles Leo had given away
→ 1 unit + 5 + 3
= 1 unit + 8
Total marbles
→ 1 unit + 1 unit + 2 + 1 unit + 5 + 1 unit + 8
= 4 units + 15

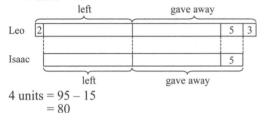

4 units = 95 − 15
      = 80
1 unit = 80 ÷ 4
      = 20
Marbles Leo had given away → 1 unit + 8
                          = 20 + 8
                          = 28

Leo gave away **28** marbles.

5   Marbles Kaden had left → 1 unit
Marbles John had left → 3 units
Marbles John gave away → 3 units + 4
Marbles Kaden gave away → 3 × (3 units + 4)
                        = 9 units + 12
Total → 1 unit + 3 units + 3 units + 4 + 9 units + 12
         _____left_____/   __given away__/
      = 16 units + 16
128 − 16 = 112
16 units = 112
  1 unit = 112 ÷ 16
        = 7
John left (3 units) → 21
John gave away (3 units + 4) → 21 + 4 = 25
Marbles John had at first → 21 + 25 = 46
John had **46** marbles at first.

6   Marbles David gave away → 1 unit
Marbles Caleb gave away → 4 units
Marbles David had left → 1 unit + 5
Marbles Caleb had left → 2 × (1 unit + 5)
                       = 2 units + 10
Marbles David had at first → 1 unit + 1 unit + 5
                           = 2 units + 5
Marbles Caleb had at first → 4 units + 2 units + 10
                           = 6 units + 10
Difference at first → Caleb had 4 units and 5 marbles
more than David at first.
37 − 5 = 32
4 units = 32
  1 unit = 32 ÷ 4
        = 8
2 units = 8 × 2
        = 16
16 + 10 = 26
Caleb had **26** marbles in the end.

7   Number of stickers John had left → 1 unit
Number of stickers John gave away → 1 unit + 10
Number of stickers Leo gave away
→ 3 × (1 unit + 10)
= 3 units + 30
Number of stickers John had at first
→ 1 unit + 1 unit + 10
= 2 units + 10
Number of stickers Leo had at first
→ 2 × (2 units + 10)
= 4 units + 20
Number of stickers Leo had at first
→ 3 units + 30 + 15
= 3 units + 45
4 units + 20 = 3 units + 45
     1 unit = 25
Stickers John gave away → 1 unit + 10
                        = 25 + 10
                        = 35
Stickers John had left → 1 unit = 25
Stickers John had at first → 35 + 25 = 60
John had **60** stickers at first.

8   Kaden had given away → 1 unit
John had given away → 4 units
John had left → 4 units + 40

Kaden left → $\frac{1}{4}$ × (4 units + 40)

$\qquad$ = 1 unit + 10

$\qquad\qquad$ given away

Total → $\overbrace{1\ \text{unit} + 4\ \text{units}}$ + $\underbrace{4\ \text{units} + 40 + 1\ \text{unit} + 10}_{\text{left}}$

$\qquad$ = 10 units + 50

350 − 50 = 300
10 units = 300
$\quad$ 1 unit = 300 ÷ 10
$\qquad\qquad$ = 30
4 units + 40 = (4 × 30) + 40
$\qquad\qquad\quad$ = 160
John had **160** marbles in the end.

9   Kaden gave away → 3 units
John gave away → 4 units
John had left → 50% × 4 units = 2 units
25% of total left in the end → 2 units
75% of total left in the end
→ 3 × 2 units
= 6 units (Kaden left in the end)

$\qquad\qquad$ given away

Total → $\overbrace{3\ \text{units} + 4\ \text{units}}$ + $\underbrace{2\ \text{units} + 6\ \text{units}}_{\text{left}}$

$\qquad$ = 15 units

15 units = 300
$\quad$ 1 unit = 300 ÷ 15
$\qquad\quad$ = 20
$\quad$ 6 units = 20 × 6
$\qquad\qquad$ = 120
Kaden had **120** marbles in the end.

10 Liam : John
$\quad$ 7 : 4
25% × 4 units = 1 unit
John left → 1 unit
John gave away → 4 units − 1 unit = 3 units
200% = $\frac{200}{100}$ = 2
Liam gave away → 2 × 3 units = 6 units
Liam left → 7 units − 6 units = 1 unit
Liam had $\frac{1}{7}$ of his magnets left.

Chapter 20   Concept – Redistribution

1   Total stickers Mr. Poh had → 15 × 8
$\qquad\qquad\qquad\qquad$ = 120
Each students in Mrs. Diaz's class got
→ 120 ÷ 12
= 10
10 − 8 = 2
A student in Class B got **2** more stickers than a student in Class A.

2   7 − 3 = 4
Each student would need 4 stickers more.
40 ÷ 4 = 10
There were 10 students.
7 × 10 = 70
Mr. Ahmad had **70** stickers.

3   5 − 3 = 2
Each student needed 2 pencils more.
24 ÷ 2 = 12
There were 12 students.
3 × 12 = 36
Mr. Poh bought **36** pencils.

4   40 + 5 = 45
7 − 4 = 3
45 ÷ 3 = 15
There were 15 students.
(4 × 15) + 40 = 100
Mr. Lee had **100** stickers.

5   140 − 20 = 120
7 − 3 = 4
120 ÷ 4 = 30
There were 30 students.
(7 × 30) + 20 = 230
Mr. Kumar bought **230** stickers.

6   260 − 20 = 240
10 − 4 = 6
240 ÷ 6 = 40
There were 40 students.
(4 × 40) − 20 = 140
Mr. Johnson had **140** stamps.

7 $9 - 5 = 4$
The last 3 students were short of 4 pencils each.
$3 \times 4 = 12$
They were short of 12 pencils in all.
$8 + 12 = 20$
$9 - 7 = 2$
$20 \div 2 = 10$
There were 10 students.
$(7 \times 10) + 8 = 78$
Mr. Poh had **78** pencils.

8 $27 - 4 = 23$
$23 \times 8 = 184$
$184 \div 4 = 46$
$27 \times 46 = 1,242$
There were **1,242** chairs in the hall.

9 $14 - 3 = 11$
Ken scored 11 marks below the average.
11 marks had to be distributed to Connie's extra and Dan's extra.
$11 - 3 = 8$ (Dan's marks above average)
$8 + 11 = 19$ (Dan's above + Ken's below)
The difference between Dan's marks and Ken's marks was **19**.

10 John $\rightarrow x + 5$
Sam $\rightarrow x + 5 - 4 = x + 1$
Total $\rightarrow x + x + 5 + x + 1 = 3x + 6$
Average $\rightarrow \dfrac{3x + 6}{3} = x + 2$
The average number of beads the three boys had was **$x + 2$**.

Review 2 – Chapters 11 to 20

1 $\boxed{} - \$17 + \$20 - \$3 = \$28$

Jessie's money at first   book   mother   cupcake   left

Work the sums backwards to find the amount she had at first.
$\$28 + \$3 = \$31$
$\$31 - \$20 = \$11$
$\$11 + \$17 = \$28$
She had **\$28** at first.

2 Total sum of three digits $\rightarrow 3 \times 5 = 15$
Sum of other two digits $\rightarrow 15 - 4 = 11$
Largest digit possible $= 9$
Smallest digit of the three $\rightarrow 11 - 9 = 2$
Largest difference between the other two digits
$\rightarrow 9 - 2 = \textbf{7}$

3 $\angle EGF = \angle EGB$ (Triangle EFG = Triangle EBG)
$\angle y + \angle EGF + \angle EGB = 180°$
$\qquad 180° - 65° - 65° = 50°$
$\qquad\qquad\qquad \angle y = \textbf{50°}$

4 $\$0.20 + \$1 = \$1.20$
The value of 1 pair of twenty-cent and one-dollar coins is **\$1.20**.
40 coins $\div$ 2 coins in each pair $= 20$ pairs
20 pairs $\times \$1.20 = \$24$
Adam has **\$24**.

5 1 group $\rightarrow 1 \times \$5$ bill $+ 3 \times \$2$ bill
$\qquad\qquad = $ Total value of $(\$5 + \$6)$
$\qquad\qquad = \$11$
$\$99 \div \$11 = 9$ (Number of groups)
$9 \times 3 = 27$
Ramesh had **27** \$2 bills in total.

6   $21 \div 4 = 5$ R 1 (5 packets of 4 and remainder of 1 egg tart)

$5 + 1 = 6$ 5×4 egg tarts = 20 egg tarts

Owen will have to buy **6** packets.

---

7   The number of gaps will always be 1 fewer than the number of pupils.

$5 - 1 = 4$ (Total number of gaps)

4×3 m = 12 m

The total distance from the first pupil to the last pupil is **12 m**.

8

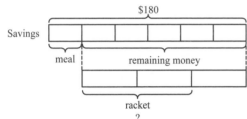

$\frac{1}{6}$ of savings → $180 \div 6 = 30$ (meal)

Remaining money $\left(\frac{5}{6}$ of savings$\right)$ → $30 \times 5 = 150$

1 unit of remaining money = $150 \div 3 = 50$

2 units of remaining money = $50 \times 2 = 100$

The cost of the badminton racket was **$100**.

---

9   Marbles John gave away → $\frac{1}{3} \times 18 = 6$

Marbles John had left → $6 + 2 = 8$

Marbles Kaden had left → $2 \times 8 = 16$

Total marbles → $6 + 8 + 16 + 18 = 48$

$\underbrace{}_{\text{John}}$ $\underbrace{}_{\text{Kaden}}$

They had **48** marbles in total at first.

---

10   $5 - 3 = 2$

Each student needed 2 more stickers from Mr. Poh.

$14 \times 2 = 28$

Mr. Poh needed to give out another 28 stickers.

$39 - 28 = 11$

Mr. Poh would have **11** stickers left.

Chapter 21 Concept – Percentage of Different Bases	

1 $100\% - 20\% = 80\%$

$80\% \rightarrow \$60$

$100\% \rightarrow \dfrac{60}{80} \times 100 = \$75$

The price of the shirt before the discount was **$75**.

---

2 $100\% - 20\% = 80\%$

$100\% - 30\% = 70\%$

$70\% \times 80\% = 56\%$

$56\% \rightarrow \$840$

$1\% \rightarrow \$840 \div 56 = \$15$

$100\% \rightarrow \$15 \times 100 = \$1,500$

Terrence had **$1,500** of savings at first.

---

3 $100\% - 20\% = 80\%$

50% of $80\% = \dfrac{50}{100} \times 80\%$

$\qquad\qquad = 40\%$

$40\% + 20\% = 60\%$

Judy gave away **60%** of her muffins.

---

4 $100\% - 20\% = 80\%$

80% of $30\% = \dfrac{80}{100} \times 30\%$

$\qquad\qquad = 24\%$

24% of the people were girls.

---

5 $100\% - 20\% = 80\%$

80% of $80\% = \dfrac{80}{100} \times 80\%$

$\qquad\qquad = 64\%$

Sam had **64%** of his money left in the end.

---

6 $20\% \rightarrow \$114$

$100\% \rightarrow 5 \times \$114 = \$570$

Joseph had $570.

$60\% \rightarrow \$570$

$100\% + 60\% = 160\%$

$160\% = \dfrac{570}{60} \times 160$

$\qquad = \$1,520$

The three of them had a total of **$1,520** at first.

---

7 Adults $\rightarrow 100\% - 10\% = 90\%$

Women $\rightarrow 30\% \times 90\% = \dfrac{30}{100} \times 90\%$

$\qquad\qquad\qquad\qquad = 27\%$

Men $\rightarrow 90\% - 27\% = 63\%$

$100\% - 60\% = 40\%$

Girls $\rightarrow 40\% \times 10\% = \dfrac{40}{100} \times 10\%$

$\qquad\qquad\qquad\quad = 4\%$

The ratio of men to girls is **63 : 4**.

---

8 Charles $\rightarrow 100\% + 15\% = 115\%$

$115\% \rightarrow \$184$

Jessie $\rightarrow 100\% = \dfrac{184}{115} \times 100$

$\qquad\qquad\qquad = \$160$

$100\% - 20\% = 80\%$

$80\% \rightarrow \$160$

$100\% \rightarrow \dfrac{160}{80} \times 100 = \$200$

Minna had **$200**.

---

9 $100\% - 10\% = 90\%$

$90\% \rightarrow \$27$

$10\% \rightarrow \$27 \div 9 = \$3$

Original price, $100\% \rightarrow \$30$

$\$27 - \$9 = \$18$

Discounted price for children, $\dfrac{18}{30} \times 100\% = 60\%$

$100\% - 60\% = 40\%$

The total percentage discount given to children below 10 is **40%**.

10 $100\% - 40\% = 60\%$
$100\% + 60\% = 160\%$
$160\% \rightarrow \$72$
Skirt, $100\% \rightarrow \dfrac{72}{160} \times 100 = \$45$
Belt, $60\% \rightarrow \dfrac{72}{160} \times 60 = \$27$
$100\% - 10\% = 90\%$
$90\% \rightarrow \$27$
Belt discount, $10\% \rightarrow \$27 \div 9 = \$3$
Skirt discount, $\$12 - \$3 = \$9$
$\$9 + \$45 = \$54$
$\dfrac{9}{54} \times 100\% \approx 16.7\%$

The percentage discount given for the skirt was approximately **16.7%**.

Chapter 22 Concept – Percentage Comparison

1 Boys $\rightarrow 100\%$
Girls $\rightarrow 100\% - 5\%$
$\quad = 95\%$
Total members $\rightarrow 100\% + 95\%$
$\quad\quad = 195\%$
$5\% \rightarrow 4$
Total members $\rightarrow \dfrac{195}{5} \times 4$
$\quad\quad = 156$
The total number of members in the club is **156**.

2 Savings $\rightarrow 100\%$
Spending $\rightarrow 180\%$
$180\% \rightarrow \$63$
$100\% + 180\% = 280\%$
Allowance $\rightarrow 280\%$ of her savings
$\dfrac{280}{180} \times \$63 = \$98$
Her allowance at the start of the month was **$98**.

3 Length $\rightarrow 100\%$
Width $\rightarrow 100\% - 60\%$
$\quad = 40\%$
Perimeter $\rightarrow 2 \times$ (Length + Width)
1 set of (Length + Width) $\rightarrow 140$ cm $\div 2$
$\quad\quad = 70$ cm
$100\% + 40\% = 140\%$
140% of length (Length + Width) $\rightarrow 70$ cm
Width (40% of length) $\rightarrow \dfrac{40}{140} \times 70$ cm
$\quad\quad = 20$ cm
The width of the rectangle is **20 cm**.

4 Class Y $\rightarrow$ 100%
Class X $\rightarrow$ 150% of Class Y
Class Y : Class X
     2 : 3
Class Z $\rightarrow$ 100%
Class X $\rightarrow$ 60% of Class Z
 Class Z : Class X
     100 : 60
       5 : 3
Class X : Class Y : Class Z
     3   :   2   :   5
Total units $\rightarrow$ 3 + 2 + 5
              = 10
10 units = 80
  1 unit = 80 ÷ 10
          = 8
 3 units = 8 × 3
          = 24
There are **24** students in Class X.

---

5 Class B $\rightarrow$ 100%
Class A $\rightarrow$ 150%
Class B : Class A = 100 : 150
                  = 2 : 3
Class C $\rightarrow$ 100%
Class B $\rightarrow$ 150% of Class C
Class C : Class B = 100 : 150
                  = 2 : 3
Class B : Class A
  ×3$\left(\begin{matrix} 2 : 3 \\ 6 : 9 \end{matrix}\right)$×3
Class C : Class B
  ×2$\left(\begin{matrix} 2 : 3 \\ 4 : 6 \end{matrix}\right)$×2
Class A : Class B : Class C
    9   :   6   :   4
The ratio is **9 : 4**.

---

6 Class B $\rightarrow$ 100%
Class A $\rightarrow$ 75%
Class C $\rightarrow$ 75% – 6
104 + 6 = 110 (If 6 students are added to Class C)
100% + 75% + 75% = 250%
250% $\rightarrow$ 110
Class A $\rightarrow \dfrac{75}{250} \times 110$
           = 33
Class C $\rightarrow$ 33 – 6
           = 27
There are **27** students in Class C.

---

7 Class $\rightarrow$ 100%
Girls $\rightarrow$ 100% – 45%
        = 55%
Girls who wear glasses : Girls who don't wear glasses
= 120 : 100
= 6 : 5
6 + 5 = 11
11 units = 55
  1 unit = 55 ÷ 11
         = 5
 6 units = 5 × 6
         = 30
30% of the class are girls who wear glasses.

---

8 Boys $\rightarrow$ 100%
Girls $\rightarrow$ 110% of boys
100% + 110% = 210%
210% $\rightarrow$ 42
Boys $\rightarrow \dfrac{100}{210} \times 42$
        = 20
Girls at first $\rightarrow$ 42 – 20
                = 22
Girls in the end $\rightarrow$ 100%
Boys $\rightarrow$ 100% + 25%
        = 125%
(Boys) 125% of girls in the end $\rightarrow$ 20
Girls in the end $\rightarrow \dfrac{100}{125} \times 20$
                = 16
Girls who went to the washroom $\rightarrow$ 22 – 16
                              = 6
6 girls went to the washroom.

                            Singapore Math Challenge Word Problems

9   Usual price of book : Discounted price of book
= 125 : 100   = 5 : 4
Discount → 5 units − 4 units = 1 unit
$\frac{1}{5} \times 100\% = 20\%$
The discount is **20%** of the usual price of the book.

10   $100\% \rightarrow 50$ km/h
$144\% \rightarrow \frac{144}{100} \times 50$
       $= 72$ km/h
6 km $\div 72$ km/h $= \frac{1}{12}$ h
          $= 5$ min
Total time → 5 min + 15 min
          $= 20$ min
          $= \frac{1}{3}$ h
15 min $= \frac{1}{4}$ h
$\frac{1}{4} \times 50 = 12.5$ km
Total distance → 12.5 km + 6 km = 18.5 km
Speed → 18.5 km $\div \frac{1}{3}$ h = 55.5 km/h
His average speed for the whole journey was
55.5 km/h.

Chapter 23   Concept – Percentage Change

1   $45 - 25 = 20$
$\frac{20}{25} \times 100\% = 80\%$
The percentage increase in the number of cars sold from March to May was **80%**.

2   Original number of teachers → 20 + 60
                          $= 80$
$100\% \rightarrow 80$ teachers
Increase in the number of teachers → 7 − 3
                          $= 4$
$\frac{4}{80} \times 100\% = 5\%$
The percentage increase in the number of teachers was **5%**.

3   <u>Ken</u>
$100\% \rightarrow 4$ units
$\frac{75}{100} \times 4$ units = 3 units
Ken gave away a total of 3 units of sweets.

    <u>Ron</u>
$100\% \rightarrow 2$ units
$\frac{50}{100} \times 2$ units = 1 unit
Ron received 1 unit of sweets from Ken.
Ivy received 2 units of sweets from Ken.

    <u>Ivy</u>
$100\% \rightarrow 5$ units
$\frac{2}{5} \times 100\% = 40\%$
The percentage increase in the number of sweets for Ivy was **40%**.

4   Before 5 male teachers left → 123 + 5 = 128
Female teachers joined → 128 − 112 = 16
20% of original female teachers → 16
Female teachers at first → $\frac{16}{20} \times 100\% = 80$
112 − 80 = 32
There were **32** male teachers at first.

5   $20\% \times \$1,000 = \$200$
5% of expenditure in November → $200
1% of expenditure in November → $40
100% of expenditure in November → $100 \times \$40$
$= \$4,000$
$\$4,000 + \$1,000 = \$5,000$
Judy's salary for each month was **$5,000**.

6   20% of expenditure in September
= 40% of savings in September
10% of expenditure in September
= 20% of savings in September
50% of expenditure in September
= 100% of savings in September
Cheryl spent was $\frac{2}{3}$ of her income in September.

7   100% (March allowance) → $40
105% (April allowance → $\frac{105}{100} \times \$40$
$= \$42$
100% (April allowance) → $42
105% (May allowance) → $\frac{105}{100} \times \$42$
$= \$44.10$
Siti's monthly allowance in May was **$44.10**.

8   100% (first test) → 75
120% (second test) → $\frac{120}{100} \times 75 = 90$
100% (second test) → 90
80% (third test) → $\frac{80}{100} \times 90 = 72$
His math score for his third test was **72**.

9   100% → Tom
$100\% - 40\% = 60\%$
Jason → 60% as many as Tom
$25\% = \frac{1}{4}$
$\frac{1}{4} \times 60\% = 15\%$
Jason in the end → $60\% - 15\%$
$= 45\%$
$100\% + 45\% = 145\%$ (Total coins in the end)
145% → 58
$45\% \to \frac{45}{145} \times 58 = 18$
Jason had **18** coins left in the end.

10 $20\% = \frac{1}{5}$
Let the original length of one side of a square be 5 units.
Original area → 5 units × 5 units
$= 25$ units^2
New length of one side of the square after the decrease
→ 5 units – 1 unit
= 4 units
New area → 4 units × 4 units
$= 16$ units^2
Decrease in area → 25 – 16
$= 9$
$\frac{9}{25} \times 100\% = 36\%$
The percentage decrease in the area of the square was **36%**.

Chapter 24 Concept – Volume of Cube

1. Volume = Length × Width × Height
   125 = 5 × 5 × 5
   The length of one edge of the cube is **5 cm**.

2. Area = Length × Width
   9 = 3 × 3
   Volume = Length × Width × Height
   = 3 × 3 × 3
   = 27
   The volume of the cube is **27 cm³**.

3. A cube has 6 square surfaces.
   Area of 6 square surfaces = 294
   Area of 1 square surface = 49
   Area = Length × Width
   49 = 7 × 7
   Volume = Length × Width × Height
   = 7 × 7 × 7
   = 343
   The volume of the cube is **343 cm³**.

4. Volume = Length × Width × Height
   729 = 9 × 9 × 9
   Area of 1 face = 9 × 9
   = 81
   Area of 6 faces = 6 × 81
   = 486
   The total surface area of the cube is **486 cm²**.

5. Volume = Length × Width × Height
   1000 = 10 × 10 × 10
   A cube has 12 edges in total.
   Total length of 12 edges = 12 × 10
   = 120
   The total length of all the edges of the cube is
   120 cm.

6. 12 edges = 96 cm
   1 edge = 8 cm
   Volume = 8 × 8 × 8
   = 512
   The volume of the cube is **512 cm³**.

7. 27 = 3 × 3 × 3
   Length of one side of Cube Y = 3 cm
   Length of one side of Cube X = 2 × 3 cm
   = 6 cm
   Volume of Cube X = 6 cm × 6 cm × 6 cm
   = 216 cm³
   The volume of the Cube X is **216 cm³**.

8. 512 = 8 × 8 × 8
   Length of one side of Cube Q = 8 cm
   Length of one side of Cube P = $\frac{1}{4}$ × 8 cm
   = 2 cm
   Volume of Cube P = 2 cm × 2 cm × 2 cm
   = 8 cm³
   Total volume of Cube P and Cube Q
   = 8 cm³ + 512 cm³
   = 520 cm³
   The total volume of Cube P and Cube Q is **520 cm³**.

9. 216 = 6 × 6 × 6
   Length of one side of Cube J = 6 cm
   75% → 6 cm
   100% → 8 cm
   Length of one side of Cube K = 8 cm
   Volume = 8 × 8 × 8
   = 512
   The volume of Cube K is **512 cm³**.

10 Volume of Cube Z = 1 unit × 1 unit × 1 unit
= 1 unit^3

Length of one side of Cube Z = 1 unit

Length of one side of Cube Y = 3 units

Volume of Cube Y = 3 units × 3 units × 3 units
= 27 units^3

The ratio of the volume of Cube Y to Cube Z is **27 : 1**.

1   In 1 hour

Kelly can clean $\frac{1}{3}$ of the fish tank.

Richard can clean $\frac{1}{6}$ of the fish tank.

Together, $\frac{1}{3} + \frac{1}{6} = \frac{2}{6} + \frac{1}{6}$
$$= \frac{3}{6}$$
$$= \frac{1}{2}$$

Kelly and Richard can clean $\frac{1}{2}$ of the fish tank in an hour if they work together.

2   In 1 hour

Kelly can clean $\frac{1}{4}$ of the fish tank.

Richard can clean $\frac{1}{6}$ of the fish tank.

$\frac{1}{4} + \frac{1}{6} = \frac{3}{12} + \frac{2}{12}$
$$= \frac{5}{12}$$

Together, they can clean $\frac{5}{12}$ of the fish tank in an hour.

3   In 1 hour

James could clean $\frac{1}{4}$ of the fridge.

Bryan could clean $\frac{1}{12}$ of the fridge.

$\frac{1}{4} + \frac{1}{12} = \frac{3}{12} + \frac{1}{12}$
$$= \frac{4}{12}$$
$$= \frac{1}{3}$$

James and Bryan could clean $\frac{1}{3}$ of the fridge in 1 hour.

$\frac{1}{3}$ of the fridge → 1 h

$\frac{3}{3}$ of the fridge → 3 h

They would need **3 h** to clean the fridge.

4 In 1 min

Kelly can clean $\frac{1}{75}$ of the set of windows.

Richard can clean $\frac{1}{50}$ of the set of windows.

$$\frac{1}{75} + \frac{1}{50} = \frac{2}{150} + \frac{3}{150}$$
$$= \frac{5}{150}$$
$$= \frac{1}{30}$$

$\frac{1}{30}$ of the set of windows → 1 min

$\frac{30}{30}$ of the set of windows → 30 min

The time taken for both of them to clean the windows together is **30 min**.

5 In 1 hour

Kelly could paint $\frac{1}{4}$ the room.

Richard could paint $\frac{1}{8}$ the room.

$$\frac{1}{4} + \frac{1}{8} = \frac{2}{8} + \frac{1}{8}$$
$$= \frac{3}{8}$$

Kelly and Richard could paint $\frac{3}{8}$ of the room if they worked together.

$\frac{3}{8}$ of the room → 1 h

$\frac{1}{8}$ of the room → $\frac{1}{3}$ h

$\frac{8}{8}$ of the room → $\frac{8}{3}$ h $= 2\frac{2}{3}$ h

They would need $2\frac{2}{3}$ **h** to paint the room.

6 In 1 hour

Emily could clean $\frac{1}{6}$ of the cabinet.

Jack and Emily could clean $\frac{1}{2}$ of the cabinet.

$$\frac{1}{2} - \frac{1}{6} = \frac{3}{6} - \frac{1}{6}$$
$$= \frac{2}{6}$$
$$= \frac{1}{3}$$

Jack could clean $\frac{1}{3}$ of the cabinet in 1 hour on his own.

$1 \times 3 = 3$

Jack would take **3 h** to clean the cabinet by himself.

7 For the same time duration, Jackson ran 120 m more than Gary.

1 min → Jackson ran 10 m more than Gary.

12 min → Jackson ran 120 m more than Gary.

12×200 m = 2400 m

The distance between point A and point B was **2400 m**.

8 1 h → Jack ran 0.8 km more than Gary.

2 h → Jack ran 1.6 km more than Gary.

10% of the journey → 1.6 km

100% of the journey → 16 km

The distance from point A to point B was **16 km**.

9 1 h → Jack could run 12 km.

$\frac{3}{4}$ h → Jack could run 9 km.

15 km − 9 km = 6 km (Distance ran by Gary)

$\frac{3}{4}$ h → Gary could run 6 km

1 h → 8 km

Gary's average speed was **8 km/h**.

10 20 min → 350 m

60 min → 3 × 350 m = 1,050 m

1,050 m = 1.05 km

The difference in their speed was **1.05 km/h**.

Chapter 26   Concept – Sum of Consecutive Numbers

1   Each pair → $1 + 20 = 21$
Total sum of 2 sets → $20 \times 21 = 420$
Sum of 1 set → $420 \div 2 = 210$
Average → $210 \div 20 = \mathbf{10.5}$

2   Each pair → $10 + 40 = 50$
Number of pairs → $40 - 10 + 1 = 31$
Total sum of 2 sets → $31 \times 50 = 1,550$
Sum of 1 set → **775**

3   Each pair → $20 + 52 = 72$
Number of even numbers from 1 to 52 → $52 \div 2$
$= 26$
Number of even numbers from 1 to 18 → $18 \div 2$
$= 9$
Number of even numbers from 20 to 52 → $26 - 9$
$= 17$
Total sum of 2 sets → $17 \times 72 = 1,224$
Sum of 1 set → 612
Average → $612 \div 17 = \mathbf{36}$

4   Total sum → $3 \times 50 = 150$

$150 - 2 - 2 - 2 = 144$
$144 \div 3 = 48$ (Smallest)
Largest → $48 + 2 + 2 = \mathbf{52}$

5   Since the numbers are consecutive, the average would be the number in the middle.
Average → $735 \div 21 = 35$ (Middle number)
$21 - 1 = 20$
$20 \div 2 = 10$
$35 - 10 = 25$
The smallest number is **25**.

6   Even → $\boxed{2} + \boxed{4} + \boxed{6} + \boxed{8} + \cdots + \boxed{44} + \boxed{46} + \boxed{48} + \boxed{50}$
Odd → $\boxed{1} + \boxed{3} + \boxed{5} + \boxed{7} + \cdots + \boxed{43} + \boxed{45} + \boxed{47} + \boxed{49}$
Difference of each pair → 1
Number of pairs → $50 \div 2 = 25$
Total difference → $25 \times 1 = \mathbf{25}$

7   Each pair → $10 + \dfrac{1}{4} = 10\dfrac{1}{4}$
Number of pairs → $10 \times 4 = 40$
Total sum of 2 sets → $40 \times 10\dfrac{1}{4} = 40 \times \dfrac{41}{4}$
$= 410$
Sum of 1 set → $410 \div 2 = \mathbf{205}$

8   Each pair → $19.9 + 0.1 = 20$
Number of pairs → $19.9 \times 10 = 199$
Total sum of 2 sets → $199 \times 20 = 3,980$
Total sum of 1 set → $3,980 \div 2 = \mathbf{1,990}$

9   See as 3 sets of $1 + 2 + 3 + \cdots + 14 + 15$.
Each pair → $1 + 15 = 16$
Number of pairs → 15
Total sum of 2 sets → $15 \times 16 = 240$
Total sum of 1 set → $240 \div 2 = 120$
Total sum of 3 sets → $3 \times 120 = \mathbf{360}$

10   Average = Middle number
Total number of numbers → $25 + 24 = 49$
$1 + 2 + 3 + \cdots + 47 + 48 + 49$
Each pair → $1 + 49 = 50$
Total sum of 2 sets → $49 \times 50 = 2,450$
Total sum of 1 set → $2,450 \div 2 = \mathbf{1,225}$

Chapter 27 Concept – Advanced Transfer

1 $\frac{2}{5}$ of Amy's money $= \frac{3}{4}$ of Ben's money

$\frac{6}{15}$ of Amy's money $= \frac{6}{8}$ of Ben's money

Amy : Ben

15 : 8

Difference at first $= 2 \times \$28$

$\qquad\qquad\qquad = \$56$

7 units $= 56$

1 unit $= 56 \div 7$

$\qquad = 8$

15 units $= 8 \times 15$

$\qquad\quad = 120$

Amy had **\$120** at first.

2 $\frac{4}{5}$ of Amy's money $= \frac{2}{7}$ of Ben's money

$\frac{4}{5}$ of Amy's money $= \frac{4}{14}$ of Ben's money

Amy : Ben

5 : 14

Difference $= \$20 + \$16$

$\qquad\qquad = \$36$

9 units $= 36$

1 unit $= 36 \div 9$

$\qquad = 4$

5 units $= 4 \times 5$

$\qquad = 20$

Amy had **\$20** at first.

3 $\frac{2}{5}$ of Ella's money $= \frac{6}{7}$ of Noah's money

$\frac{6}{15}$ of Ella's money $= \frac{6}{7}$ of Noah's money

Ella : Noah

15 : 7

Difference at first $= \$20 + \$36$

$\qquad\qquad\qquad = \$56$

8 units $= 56$

1 unit $= 56 \div 8$

$\qquad = 7$

15 units $= 7 \times 15$

$\qquad\quad = 105$

$\$105 - \$36 = \$69$

Ella had **\$69** in the end.

4 $\frac{1}{2}$ of Amy's money $= \frac{3}{4}$ of Ben's money

$\frac{3}{6}$ of Amy's money $= \frac{3}{4}$ of Ben's money

Amy : Ben

6 : 4

3 : 2

Difference at first $\rightarrow \$6 + \$5 + \$5$

$\qquad\qquad\qquad\quad = \$16$

1 unit $= \$16$

2 units $= \$16 \times 2$

$\qquad\quad = \$32$

Ben had **\$32** at first.

5 $\frac{3}{5}$ of Amy's money $= \frac{4}{5}$ of Ben's money

$\frac{12}{20}$ of Amy's money $= \frac{12}{15}$ of Ben's money

Amy : Ben

20 : 15

4 : 3

Difference at first $\rightarrow$ 1 unit $= \$100 - \$30 - \$30$

$\qquad\qquad\qquad\qquad\qquad\quad = \$40$

Ben $\rightarrow$ 3 units $= \$40 \times 3$

$\qquad\qquad\qquad\quad = \$120$

Ben had **\$120** at first.

6 $\frac{1}{3}$ of Mia's money $= \frac{4}{5}$ of Alan's money

$\frac{4}{12}$ of Mia's money $= \frac{4}{5}$ of Alan's money

Mia : Alan

12 : 5

Money given by Mia to Alan $\rightarrow \$18 - \$4$

$\qquad\qquad\qquad\qquad\qquad\quad = \$14$

Difference $\rightarrow$ 7 units $= 2 \times \$14$

$\qquad\qquad\qquad\qquad = \$28$

1 unit $= 28 \div 7$

$\qquad = 4$

Mia $\rightarrow$ 12 units $= 4 \times 12$

$\qquad\qquad\qquad\quad = 48$

Mia had **\$48** at first.

7 $\frac{3}{5}$ of Amy's money = $2 \times \frac{1}{4}$ of Ben's money

$\frac{3}{5}$ of Amy's money = $\frac{2}{4}$ of Ben's money

$\frac{3}{5}$ of Amy's money = $\frac{1}{2}$ of Ben's money

$\frac{3}{5}$ of Amy's money = $\frac{3}{6}$ of Ben's money

Amy : Ben
   5 : 6
Difference at first → $26 – $3 – $3
                  = $20

1 unit = $20
6 units = $20 × 6
      = $120
Ben had **$120** at first.

8 $\frac{1}{5}$ of Amy's money = $\frac{1}{3}$ of Ben's money + $12

$\frac{3}{5}$ of Amy's money = $\frac{3}{3}$ of Ben's money + $36

Difference at first → $\frac{2}{5}$ of Amy's money + $36

Difference at first → $50 × 2
                  = $100

$\frac{2}{5}$ of Amy's money + $36 = $100

$100 – $36 = $64

$\frac{2}{5}$ of Amy's money = $64

$\frac{1}{5}$ of Amy's money = $32

Amy's money = $32 × 5
           = $160

Amy had **$160** at first.

9 $\frac{2}{5}$ of Zoe's money = $\frac{2}{3}$ of Luke's money + $12

$\frac{1}{5}$ of Zoe's money = $\frac{1}{3}$ of Luke's money + $6

$\frac{3}{5}$ of Zoe's money = $\frac{3}{3}$ of Luke's money + $18

Difference → $\frac{2}{5}$ of Zoe's money + $18

Difference → $50 × 2
          = $100

$100 – $18 = $82

$\frac{2}{5}$ of Zoe's money = $82

$\frac{2}{3}$ of Luke's money = $82 – 12
                           = $70

$\frac{1}{3}$ of Luke's money = $70 ÷ 2
                           = $35

Luke's money = $35 × 3
            = $105
Luke had **$105** at first.

10 50% of Amy's money = 75% of Ben's money

$\frac{1}{2}$ of Amy's money = $\frac{3}{4}$ of Ben's money

$\frac{3}{6}$ of Amy's money = $\frac{3}{4}$ of Ben's money

Amy : Ben
   6 : 4
   3 : 2
Difference in the end → 1 unit = $36 × 2
                            = $72

Total at first → 5 units = $72 × 5
                      = $360

(Total at first = total in the end, as no money was given away to a third party)
Amy and Ben had **$360** in total at first.